PROFILES IN COURAGE

Books by John F. Kennedy

THE BURDEN AND THE GLORY
(*edited by Allan Nevins*)

TO TURN THE TIDE
(*edited by John W. Gardner*)

THE STRATEGY OF PEACE
(*edited by Allan Nevins*)

PROFILES IN COURAGE

WHY ENGLAND SLEPT

JOHN F. KENNEDY

PROFILES IN COURAGE

Memorial Edition

Special foreword by Robert F. Kennedy

PERENNIAL LIBRARY
Harper & Row, Publishers
NEW YORK

The publisher's share of royalties on this Perennial Library edition will be contributed to the John F. Kennedy Memorial Award in biography and history (including current history).

Profiles in Courage was originally published by Harper & Brothers in 1956.

First PERENNIAL LIBRARY edition published 1964 by Harper & Row, Publishers, Incorporated, New York.

SBN: 06-080001-1

LIBRARY OF CONGRESS CATALOG CARD NUMBER: 64-16194

16-74

Contents

Foreword to the Memorial Edition

Courage is the virtue that President Kennedy most admired. He sought out those people who had demonstrated in some way, whether it was on a battlefield or a baseball diamond, in a speech or fighting for a cause, that they had courage, that they would stand up, that they could be counted on.

That is why this book so fitted his personality, his beliefs. It is a study of men who, at risk to themselves, their futures, even the well-being of their children, stood fast for principle. It was toward that ideal that he modeled his life. And this in time gave heart to others.

As Andrew Jackson said, "One man with courage makes a majority." That is the effect President Kennedy had on others.

President Kennedy would have been forty-seven in May of 1964. At least one half of the days that he spent on this earth were days of intense physical pain. He had scarlet fever when he was very young, and serious back trouble when he was older. In between he had almost every other conceivable ailment. When we were growing up together we used to laugh about the great risk a mosquito took in biting Jack Kennedy—with some of his blood the mosquito was almost sure to die. He was in Chelsea Naval Hospital for an extended period of time after the war, had a major and painful operation on his back in 1955, campaigned on crutches in 1958. In 1951 on a trip we took around the world he became ill. We flew to the military hospital in Okinawa and he had a temperature of over 106 degrees. They didn't think he would live.

But during all this time, I never heard him complain. I never heard him say anything that would indicate that he felt God had dealt with him unjustly. Those who knew him well would know he was suffering only because his face was a little whiter, the lines around his eyes were a little deeper, his words a little sharper. Those who did not know him well detected nothing.

He didn't complain about his problem, so why should I complain about mine—that is how one always felt.

When he battled against illness, when he fought in the war, when he ran for the Senate, when he stood up against powerful interests in Massachusetts to fight for the St. Lawrence Seaway, when he fought for a labor reform act in 1959, when he entered the West Virginia primary in 1960, when he debated Lyndon Johnson at the Democratic Convention in Los Angeles with no advance notice, when he took the blame completely on himself for the failure at the Bay of Pigs, when he fought the steel companies, when he stood up at Berlin in 1961 and then again in 1962 for the freedom of that city, when he forced the withdrawal of the Soviet missiles from Cuba, when he spoke and fought for equal rights for all our citizens, and hundreds of other things both big and small, he was reflecting what is the best in the human being.

He was demonstrating conviction, courage, a desire to help others who needed help, and true and genuine love for his country.

Because of his efforts, the mentally retarded and the mentally ill will have a better chance, the young a greater opportunity to be educated and live with dignity and self-respect, the ill to be cared for, the world to live in peace.

President Kennedy had only a thousand days in the White House instead of three thousand days, yet so much was accomplished. Still so much needs to be done.

This book tells the stories of men who in their own time recognized what needed to be done—and did it. President Kennedy was fond of quoting Dante that "the hottest places in Hell are reserved for those who, in a time of great moral crisis, maintain their neutrality."

If there is a lesson from the lives of the men John Kennedy depicts in this book, if there is a lesson from his life and from his death, it is that in this world of ours none of us can afford to be lookers-on, the critics standing on the sidelines.

Thomas Carlyle wrote, "The courage we desire and prize is not the courage to die decently but to live manfully."

On the morning of his death, President Kennedy called former Vice President John Nance Garner to pay his respects. It was Mr. Garner's ninety-fifth birthday. When Mr. Garner first came to Washington the total federal budget was less than 500 million dollars. President Kennedy was administering a budget of just under 100 billion dollars.

President Kennedy's grandmother was living in Boston when President Kennedy was assassinated. She was also alive the year President Lincoln was shot.

We are a young country. We are growing and expanding until it appears that this planet will no longer contain us. We have problems now that people fifty, even ten years ago, would not have dreamed would have to be faced.

The energies and talents of all of us are needed to meet the challenges—the internal ones of our cities, our farms, ourselves—to be successful in the fight for freedom around the globe, in the battles against illiteracy, hunger and disease. Pleasantries, self-satisfied mediocrity will serve us badly. We need the best of many—not of just a few. We must strive for excellence.

Lord Tweedsmuir, one of the President's favorite authors, wrote in his autobiography: "Public life is the crown of a career, and to young men it is the worthiest ambition. Politics is still the greatest and most honorable adventure."

It has been fashionable in many places to look down on politics, on those in Government. President Kennedy, I think, changed that and altered the public conception of Government. He certainly did for those who participated. But, however we feel about politics, the arena of Government is where the decisions will be made which will affect not only all our destinies but the future of our children born and unborn.

At the time of the Cuban missile crisis last year, we discussed the possibility of war, a nuclear exchange, and talked about being killed—the latter at that time seemed so unimportant, almost frivolous. The one matter which really was of concern to him and truly had meaning and made that time much more fearful than it would otherwise have been was the specter of the death of the children of this country and around the world—the young people who had no part and knew nothing of the confrontation, but whose lives would be snuffed out like everyone else's. They would never have been given a chance to make a decision, to vote in an election, to run for office, to lead a revolution, to determine their own destinies.

We, our generation, had. And the great tragedy was that if we erred, we erred not just for ourselves, our futures, our homes, our country, but for the lives, futures, homes and countries of those who never had been given an opportunity to play a role, to vote "aye" or "nay," to make themselves felt.

Bonar Law said, "There is no such thing as inevitable war. If war comes it will be from failure of human wisdom."

It is true. It is human wisdom that is needed not just on our side but on all sides. I might add that if wisdom had not been demonstrated by the American President and also by Premier Khrushchev, then the world as we know it would have been destroyed.

But there will be future Cubas. There will be future crises. We have the problems of the hungry, the neglected, the poor and the downtrodden. They must receive more help. And just as solutions had to be found in October of 1962, answers must be found for these other problems that still face us. So that wisdom is needed still.

John Quincy Adams, Daniel Webster, Sam Houston, Thomas Hart Benton, Edmund G. Ross, Lucius Quintus Cincinnatus Lamar, George Norris and Robert Taft imparted a heritage to us. They came, they left their mark, and this country was not the same because these men had lived. By how much the good of what they did and deeded to us was cherished, nurtured and encouraged, by so much did the country and all of us gain.

And so it is also for John F. Kennedy. Like these others, his life had an import, meant something to the country while he was alive. More significant, however, is what we do with what is left, with what has been started. It was his conviction, like Plato's, that the definition of citizenship in a democracy is participation in Government and that, as Francis Bacon wrote, it is "left only to God and to the angels to be lookers on." It was his conviction that a democracy with this effort by its people must and can face its problems, that it must show patience, restraint, compassion, as well as wisdom and strength and courage, in the struggle for solutions which are very rarely easy to find.

It was his conviction that we should do so successfully because the courage of those who went before us in this land exists in the present generation of Americans.

"We dare not forget today that we are the heirs of that first revolution. Let the word go forth from this time and place, to friend and foe alike, that the torch has been passed to a new generation of Americans—born in this century, tempered by war, disciplined by a hard and bitter peace, proud of our ancient heritage—and unwilling to witness or permit the slow undoing of those human rights to which this nation has always been committed, and to which we are committed today at home and around the world."

This book is not just the stories of the past but a book of hope and confidence for the future. What happens to the country, to the world, depends on what we do with what others have left us.

—ROBERT F. KENNEDY

December 18, 1963

Preface

Since first reading—long before I entered the Senate—an account of John Quincy Adams and his struggle with the Federalist party, I have been interested in the problems of political courage in the face of constituent pressures, and the light shed on those problems by the lives of past statesmen. A long period of hospitalization and convalescence following a spinal operation in October, 1954, gave me my first opportunity to do the reading and research necessary for this project.

I am not a professional historian; and, although all errors of fact and judgment are exclusively my own, I should like to acknowledge with sincere gratitude those who assisted me in the preparation of this volume.

I owe a special debt of gratitude to an outstanding American institution—the Library of Congress. Throughout the many months of my absence from Washington, the Legislative Reference and Loan Divisions of the Library fulfilled all of my requests for books with amazing promptness and cheerful courtesy. Milton Kaplan and Virginia Daiker of the Prints and Photos Division were most helpful in suggesting possible illustrations. Dr. George Galloway, and particularly Dr. William R. Tansill, of the Library Staff, made important contributions to the selection of examples for inclusion in the book, as did Arthur Krock of the *New York Times* and Professor James McGregor Burns of Williams College.

Professor John Bystrom of the University of Minnesota, former Nebraska Attorney General C. A. Sorensen, and the Honorable Hugo Srb, Clerk of the Nebraska State Legislature, were helpful in providing previously unpublished correspondence of George Norris and pertinent documents of the Nebraska State Legislature.

Professor Jules Davids of Georgetown University assisted materially in the preparation of several chapters, as did my able friend James M. Landis, who delights in bringing the precision of the lawyer to the mysteries of history.

Chapters II through X were greatly improved by the criticisms of Professors Arthur N. Holcombe and Arthur M. Schlesinger, Jr., both of Harvard; and Professor Walter Johnson of the University of Chicago. The editorial suggestions, understanding cooperation and initial encouragement which I received from Evan Thomas of Harper & Brothers made this book possible.

To Gloria Liftman and Jane Donovan, my thanks for their efforts above and beyond the call of duty in typing and retyping this manuscript.

The greatest debt is owed to my research associate, Theodore C. Sorensen, for his invaluable assistance in the assembly and preparation of the material upon which this book is based.

This book would not have been possible without the encouragement, assistance and criticisms offered from the very beginning by my wife Jacqueline, whose help during all the days of my convalescence I cannot ever adequately acknowledge.

—John F. Kennedy

1955

TO MY WIFE

He well knows what snares are spread about his path, from personal animosity . . . and possibly from popular delusion. But he has put to hazard his ease, his security, his interest, his power, even his . . . popularity . . . He is traduced and abused for his supposed motives. He will remember that obloquy is a necessary ingredient in the composition of all true glory: he will remember . . . that calumny and abuse are essential parts of triumph . . . He may live long, he may do much. But here is the summit. He never can exceed what he does this day.

—Edmund Burke's eulogy of Charles James Fox
for his attack upon the
tyranny of the East India Company—
House of Commons, December 1, 1783

I

COURAGE AND POLITICS

This is a book about that most admirable of human virtues—courage. "Grace under pressure," Ernest Hemingway defined it. And these are the stories of the pressures experienced by eight United States Senators and the grace with which they endured them—the risks to their careers, the unpopularity of their courses, the defamation of their characters, and sometimes, but sadly only sometimes, the vindication of their reputations and their principles.

A nation which has forgotten the quality of courage which in the past has been brought to public life is not as likely to insist upon or reward that quality in its chosen leaders today—and in fact we have forgotten. We may remember how John Quincy Adams became President through the political schemes of Henry Clay, but we have forgotten how, as a young man, he gave up a promising Senatorial career to stand by the nation. We may remember Daniel Webster for his subservience to the National Bank throughout much of his career, but we have forgotten his sacrifice for the national good at the close of that career. We do not remember—and possibly we do not care.

"People don't give a damn," a syndicated columnist told millions of readers not so many years ago, "what the average Senator or Congressman says. The reason they don't care is that they know what you hear in Congress is 99% tripe, ignorance and demagoguery and not to be relied upon. . . ."

Earlier a member of the Cabinet had recorded in his diary:

> While I am reluctant to believe in the total depravity of the Senate, I place but little dependence on the honesty and truthfulness of a large portion of the Senators. A majority of them are small lights, mentally weak, and wholly unfit to be Senators. Some are vulgar demagogues . . . some are men of wealth who have purchased their position . . . [some are] men of narrow intellect, limited comprehension, and low partisan prejudice. . . .

And still earlier a member of the Senate itself told his colleagues that "the confidence of the people is departing from us, owing to our unreasonable delays."

The Senate knows that many Americans today share these sentiments. Senators, we hear, must be politicians—and politicians must be concerned only with winning votes, not with statesmanship or courage. Mothers may still want their favorite sons to grow up to be President, but, according to a famous Gallup poll of some years ago, they do not want them to become politicians in the process.

Does this current rash of criticism and disrespect mean the quality of the Senate has declined? Certainly not. For of the three statements quoted above, the first was made in the twentieth century, the second in the nineteenth and the third in the eighteenth (when the first Senate, barely underway, was debating where the Capitol should be located).

Does it mean, then, that the Senate can no longer boast of men of courage?

Walter Lippmann, after nearly half a century of careful observation, rendered in his recent book a harsh judgment both on the politician and the electorate:

> With exceptions so rare they are regarded as miracles of nature, successful democratic politicians are insecure and intimidated men. They advance politically only as they placate, appease, bribe, seduce, bamboozle, or otherwise manage to manipulate the demanding threatening elements in their constituencies. The decisive consideration is not whether the proposition is good but whether it is popular—not whether it will work well and prove itself, but whether the active-talking constituents like it immediately.

I am not so sure, after nearly ten years of living and working in the midst of "successful democratic politicians," that they are all "insecure and intimidated men." I am convinced that the complication of public business and the competition for the public's attention have obscured innumerable acts of political courage—large and small—performed almost daily in the Senate Chamber. I am convinced that the decline—if there has been a decline—has been less in the Senate than in the public's appreciation of the art of politics, of the nature and necessity for compromise and balance, and of the nature of the Senate as a legislative chamber. And, finally, I am convinced that we have criticized those who have followed the crowd—and at the same time criticized those who have defied it—because we have not fully understood the responsibility of a Senator to his constituents or recognized the difficulty facing a politician conscientiously desiring, in Webster's words, "to push [his] skiff from the shore alone" into a hostile and turbulent sea. Perhaps if the American people more fully comprehended the terrible pressures which discourage acts of political courage, which drive a Senator to abandon or subdue his conscience, then they might be less critical of those who take the easier road—and more appreciative of those still able to follow the path of courage.

The *first* pressure to be mentioned is a form of pressure rarely recognized by the general public. Americans want to be liked—and Senators are no exception. They are by nature—and of necessity—social animals. We enjoy the comradeship and approval of our friends and colleagues. We prefer praise to abuse, popularity to contempt. Realizing that the path of the conscientious insurgent must frequently be a lonely one, we are anxious to get along with our fellow legislators, our fellow members of the club, to abide by the clubhouse rules and patterns, not to pursue a unique and independent course which would embarrass or irritate the other members. We realize, moreover, that our influence in the club—and the extent to which we can accomplish our objecttives and those of our constituents—are dependent in some measure on the esteem with which we are regarded by other Senators. "The way to get along," I was told when I entered Congress, "is to go along."

Going along means more than just good fellowship—it includes the use of compromise, the sense of things possible. We should not be too hasty in condemning all compromise as bad morals. For politics and legislation are not matters for inflexible principles or unattainable ideals. Politics, as John Morley has acutely observed, "is a field where action is one long second best, and where the choice constantly lies between two blunders"; and legislation, under the democratic way of life and the Federal system of Government, requires compromise between the desires of each individual and group and those around them. Henry Clay, who should have known, said compromise was the cement that held the Union together:

> All legislation . . . is founded upon the principle of mutual concession. . . . Let him who elevates himself above

humanity, above its weaknesses, its infirmities, its wants, its necessities, say, if he pleases, "I never will compromise"; but let no one who is not above the frailties of our common nature disdain compromise.

It is compromise that prevents each set of reformers—the wets and the drys, the one-worlders and the isolationists, the vivisectionists and the anti-vivisectionists—from crushing the group on the extreme opposite end of the political spectrum. The fanatics and extremists and even those conscientiously devoted to hard and fast principles are always disappointed at the failure of their Government to rush to implement all of their principles and to denounce those of their opponents. But the legislator has some responsibility to conciliate those opposing forces within his state and party and to represent them in the larger clash of interests on the national level; and he alone knows that there are few if any issues where all the truth and all the right and all the angels are on one side.

Some of my colleagues who are criticized today for lack of forthright principles—or who are looked upon with scornful eyes as compromising "politicians"—are simply engaged in the fine art of conciliating, balancing and interpreting the forces and factions of public opinion, an art essential to keeping our nation united and enabling our Government to function. Their consciences may direct them from time to time to take a more rigid stand for principle—but their intellects tell them that a fair or poor bill is better than no bill at all, and that only through the give-and-take of compromise will any bill receive the successive approval of the Senate, the House, the President and the nation.

But the question is how we will compromise and with whom. For it is easy to seize upon unnecessary concessions, not as means of legitimately resolving conflicts but as methods of "going along."

There were further implications in the warning that I

should "go along"—implications of the rewards that would follow fulfillment of my obligation to follow the party leadership whom I had helped select. All of us in the Congress are made fully aware of the importance of party unity (what sins have been committed in that name!) and the adverse effect upon our party's chances in the next election which any rebellious conduct might bring. Moreover, in these days of Civil Service, the loaves and fishes of patronage available to the legislator —for distribution to those earnest campaigners whose efforts were inspired by something more than mere conviction—are comparatively few; and he who breaks the party's ranks may find that there are suddenly none at all. Even the success of legislation in which he is interested depends in part on the extent to which his support of his party's programs has won him the assistance of his party's leaders. Finally, the Senator who follows the independent course of conscience is likely to discover that he has earned the disdain not only of his colleagues in the Senate and his associates in his party but also that of the all-important contributors to his campaign fund.

It is thinking of the next campaign—the desire to be re-elected—that provides the *second* pressure on the conscientious Senator. It should not automatically be assumed that this is a wholly selfish motive—although it is not unnatural that those who have chosen politics as their profession should seek to continue their careers—for Senators who go down to defeat in a vain defense of a single principle will not be on hand to fight for that or any other principle in the future.

Defeat, moreover, is not only a setback for the Senator himself—he is also obligated to consider the effect upon the party he supports, upon the friends and supporters who have "gone out on a limb" for him or invested their savings in his career, and even upon the wife and children whose happiness and security—often depending at least in part upon his success in office—may mean more to him than anything else.

Where else, in a non-totalitarian country, but in the political profession is the individual expected to sacrifice all—including his own career—for the national good? In private life, as in industry, we expect the individual to advance his own enlightened self-interest—within the limitations of the law—in order to achieve over-all progress. But in public life we expect individuals to sacrifice their private interests to permit the national good to progress.

In no other occupation but politics is it expected that a man will sacrifice honors, prestige and his chosen career on a single issue. Lawyers, businessmen, teachers, doctors, all face difficult personal decisions involving their integrity—but few, if any, face them in the glare of the spotlight as do those in public office. Few, if any, face the same dread finality of decision that confronts a Senator facing an important call of the roll. He may want more time for his decision—he may believe there is something to be said for both sides—he may feel that a slight amendment could remove all difficulties—but when that roll is called he cannot hide, he cannot equivocate, he cannot delay—and he senses that his constituency, like the Raven in Poe's poem, is perched there on his Senate desk, croaking "Nevermore" as he casts the vote that stakes his political future.

Few Senators "retire to Pocatello" by choice. The virus of Potomac Fever, which rages everywhere in Washington, breeds nowhere in more virulent form than on the Senate floor. The prospect of forced retirement from "the most exclusive club in the world," the possibilities of giving up the interesting work, the fascinating trappings and the impressive prerogatives of Congressional office, can cause even the most courageous politician serious loss of sleep. Thus, perhaps without realizing it, some Senators tend to take the easier, less troublesome path to harmonize or rationalize what at first appears to be a conflict between their conscience—or the result of their deliberations—and the majority opinion of their constituents. Such Senators are not political cowards—they have simply developed the habit of sincerely reaching conclusions inevitably in accordance with popular opinion.

Still other Senators have not developed that habit—they have neither conditioned nor subdued their consciences—but they feel, sincerely and without cynicism, that they must leave considerations of conscience aside if they are to be effective. The profession of politics, they would agree with political writer Frank Kent, is not immoral, simply nonmoral:

> Probably the most important single accomplishment for the politically ambitious is the fine art of seeming to say something without doing so. . . . The important thing is not to be on the right side of the current issue but on the popular side . . . regardless of your own convictions or of the facts. This business of getting the votes is a severely practical one into which matters of morality, of right and wrong, should not be allowed to intrude.

And Kent quotes the advice allegedly given during the 1920 campaign by former Senator Ashurst of Arizona to his colleague Mark Smith:

> Mark, the great trouble with you is that you refuse to be a demagogue. You will not submerge your principles in order to get yourself elected. *You must learn that there are times when a man in public life is compelled to rise above his principles.*

Not all Senators would agree—but few would deny that the desire to be re-elected exercises a strong brake on independent courage.

The *third* and most significant source of pressures which discourage political courage in the conscientious Senator or Congressman—and practically all of the problems described in this chapter apply equally to members of both Houses—is the pressure of his constituency, the interest groups, the organized letter writers, the economic blocs and even the average voter. To cope with such pressures, to defy them or even to satisfy them, is a formidable task. All of us occasionally have the urge to follow the example of Congressman John Steven McGroarty of California, who wrote a constituent in 1934:

> One of the countless drawbacks of being in Congress is that I am compelled to receive impertinent letters from a jackass like you in which you say I promised to have the Sierra Madre mountains reforested and I have been in Congress two months and haven't done it. Will you please take two running jumps and go to hell.

Fortunately or unfortunately, few follow that urge—but the provocation is there—not only from unreasonable letters and impossible requests, but also from hopelessly inconsistent demands and endlessly unsatisfied grievances.

In my office today, for example, was a delegation representing New England textile mills, an industry essential to our prosperity. They want the tariff lowered on the imported wool they buy from Australia and they want the tariff raised on the finished woolen goods imported from England with which they must compete. One of my Southern colleagues told me that a similar group visited him not long ago with the same request—but further urging that he take steps to (1) end the low-wage competition from Japan and (2) prevent the Congress from ending—through a higher minimum wage—the low-wage advantage they themselves enjoy to the dismay of my constituents. Only yesterday two groups called me off the Senate floor—the first was a group of businessmen seeking to have a local Government activity closed as unfair competition for private enterprise; and the other was a group representing the men who work in the Government installation and who are worried about their jobs.

All of us in the Senate meet endless examples of such conflicting pressures, which only reflect the inconsistencies inevitable in our complex economy. If we tell our constituents frankly that we can do nothing, they feel we are unsympathetic or inadequate. If we try and fail—usually meeting a counteraction from other Senators representing other interests—they say we are like all the rest of the politicians. All we can do is retreat into the Cloakroom and weep on the shoulder of a sympathetic colleague—or go home and snarl at our wives.

We may tell ourselves that these pressure groups and letter writers represent only a small percentage of the voters—and this is true. But they are the articulate few whose views cannot be ignored and who constitute the greater part of our contacts with the public at large, whose opinions we cannot know, whose vote we must obtain and yet who in all probability have a limited idea of what we are trying to do. (One Senator, since retired, said that he voted with the special interests on every issue, hoping that by election time all of them added together would constitute nearly a majority that would remember him favorably, while the other members of the public would never know about—much less remember—his vote against their welfare. It is reassuring to know that this seemingly unbeatable formula did not work in his case.)

These, then, are some of the pressures which confront a man of conscience. He cannot ignore the pressure groups, his constituents, his party, the comradeship of his colleagues, the needs of his family, his own pride in office, the necessity for compromise and the importance of remaining in office. He must judge for himself which path to choose, which step will most help or hinder the ideals to which he is committed. He realizes that once he begins to weigh each issue in terms of his chances for re-election, once he begins to compromise away his principles on one issue after another for fear that to do otherwise would halt his career and prevent future fights for principle, then he has lost the very freedom of conscience which justifies his continuance in office. But to decide at which point and on which issue he will risk his career is a difficult and soul-searching decision.

* * *

But this is no real problem, some will say. Always do what is right, regardless of whether it is popular. Ignore the pressures, the temptations, the false compromises.

That is an easy answer—but it is easy only for those who do not bear the responsibilities of elected office. For more is involved than pressure, politics and personal ambitions. Are we rightfully entitled to ignore the demands of our constituents even if we are able and willing to do so? We have noted the pressures that make political courage a difficult course—let us turn now to those Constitutional and more theoretical obligations which cast doubt upon the propriety of such a course—obligations to our state and section, to our party and, above all, to our constituents.

The primary responsibility of a Senator, most people assume, is to represent the views of his state. Ours is a Federal system—a Union of relatively sovereign states whose needs differ greatly—and my Constitutional obligations as Senator would thus appear to require me to represent the interests of my state. Who will speak for Massachusetts if her own Senators do not? Her rights and even her identity become submerged. Her equal representation in Congress is lost. Her aspirations, however much they may from time to time be in the minority, are denied that equal opportunity to be heard to which all minority views are entitled.

Any Senator need not look very long to realize that his

colleagues are representing *their* local interests. And if such interests are ever to be abandoned in favor of the national good, let the constituents—not the Senator—decide when and to what extent. For he is their agent in Washington, the protector of their rights, recognized by the Vice President in the Senate Chamber as "the Senator from Massachusetts" or "the Senator from Texas."

But when all of this is said and admitted, we have not yet told the full story. For in Washington we are "United States Senators" and members of the Senate of the United States as well as Senators from Massachusetts and Texas. Our oath of office is administered by the Vice President, not by the Governors of our respective states; and we come to Washington, to paraphrase Edmund Burke, not as hostile ambassadors or special pleaders for our state or section, in opposition to advocates and agents of other areas, but as members of the deliberative assembly of one nation with one interest. Of course, we should not ignore the needs of our area—nor could we easily as products of that area—but none could be found to look out for the national interest if local interests wholly dominated the role of each of us.

There are other obligations in addition to those of state and region—the obligations of the party whose pressures have already been described. Even if I can disregard those pressures, do I not have an obligation to go along with the party that placed me in office? We believe in this country in the principle of party responsibility, and we recognize the necessity of adhering to party platforms—if the party label is to mean anything to the voters. Only in this way can our basically two-party nation avoid the pitfall of multiple splinter parties, whose purity and rigidity of principle, I might add—if I may suggest a sort of Gresham's Law of politics—increase inversely with the size of their membership.

And yet we cannot permit the pressures of party responsibility to submerge on every issue the call of personal responsibility. For the party which, in its drive for unity, discipline and success, ever decides to exclude new ideas, independent conduct or insurgent members, is in danger. In the words of Senator Albert Beveridge:

> A party can live only by growing, intolerance of ideas brings its death. . . . An organization that depends upon reproduction only for its vote, son taking the place of father, is not a political party, but a Chinese tong; not citizens brought together by thought and conscience, but an Indian tribe held together by blood and prejudice.

The two-party system remains not because both are rigid but because both are flexible. The Republican party when I entered Congress was big enough to hold, for example, both Robert Taft and Wayne Morse—and the Democratic side of the Senate in which I now serve can happily embrace, for example, both Harry Byrd and Wayne Morse.

Of course, both major parties today seek to serve the national interest. They would do so in order to obtain the broadest base of support, if for no nobler reason. But when party and officeholder differ as to how the national interest is to be served, we must place first the responsibility we owe not to our party or even to our constituents but to our individual consciences.

But it is a little easier to dismiss one's obligations to local interests and party ties than to face squarely the problem of one's responsibility to the will of his constituents. A Senator who avoids this responsibility would appear to be accountable to no one, and the basic safeguards of our democratic system would thus have vanished. He is no longer representative in the true sense, he has violated his public trust, he has betrayed the confidence demonstrated by those who voted for him to carry out their views. "Is the creature," as John Tyler asked the House of Representatives in his maiden speech, "to set himself in opposition to his Creator? Is the servant to disobey the wishes of his master?"

How can he be regarded as representing the people when he speaks, not their language, but his own? He ceases to be their representative when he does so, and represents himself alone.

In short, according to this school of thought, if I am to be properly responsive to the will of my constituents, it is my duty to place their principles, not mine, above all else. This may not always be easy, but it nevertheless is the essence of democracy, faith in the wisdom of the people and their views. To be sure, the people will make mistakes—they will get no better government than they deserve—but that is far better than the representative of the people arrogating for himself the right to say he knows better than they what is good for them. Is he not chosen, the argument closes, to vote as they would vote were they in his place?

It is difficult to accept such a narrow view of the role of United States Senator—a view that assumes the people of Massachusetts sent me to Washington to serve merely as a seismograph to record shifts in popular opinion. I reject this view not because I lack faith in the "wisdom of the people," but because this concept of democracy actually puts too little faith in the people. Those who would deny the obligation of the representative to be bound by every impulse of the electorate —regardless of the conclusions his own deliberations direct—do trust in the wisdom of the people. They have faith in their ultimate sense of justice, faith in their ability to honor courage and respect judgment, and faith that in the long run they will act unselfishly for the good of the nation. It is that kind of faith on which democracy is based, not simply the often frustrated hope that public opinion will at all times under all circumstances promptly identify itself with the public interest.

The voters selected us, in short, because they had confidence in our judgment and our ability to exercise that judgment from a position where we could determine what were their own best interests, as a part of the nation's interests. This may mean that we must on occasion lead, inform, correct and sometimes even ignore constituent opinion, if we are to exercise fully that judgment for which we were elected. But acting without selfish motive or private bias, those who follow the dictates of an intelligent conscience are not aristocrats, demagogues, eccentrics or callous politicians insensitive to the feelings of the public. They expect—and not without considerable trepidation—their constituents to be the final judges of the wisdom of their course; but they have faith that those constituents—today, tomorrow or even in another generation—will at least respect the principles that motivated their independent stand.

If their careers are temporarily or even permanently buried under an avalanche of abusive editorials, poison-pen letters, and opposition votes at the polls—as they sometimes are, for that is the risk they take—they await the future with hope and confidence, aware of the fact that the voting public frequently suffers from what ex-Congressman T. V. Smith called the lag "between our way of thought and our way of life." Smith compared it to the subject of the anonymous poem:

> There was a dachshund once, so long
> He hadn't any notion
> How long it took to notify
> His tail of his emotion;
> And so it happened, while his eyes
> Were filled with woe and sadness,
> His little tail went wagging on
> Because of previous gladness.

Moreover, I question whether any Senator, before we vote on a measure, can state with certainty exactly how the majority of his constituents feel on the issue as it is presented to the Senate. All of us in the Senate live in an iron lung—the iron lung of politics, and it is no easy task to emerge from that rarefied atmosphere in order to breathe the same fresh air our constituents breathe. It is difficult, too, to see in person an appreciable number of voters besides those professional hangers-on and vocal elements who gather about the politician on a trip home. In Washington I frequently find myself believing that forty or fifty letters, six visits from professional politicians and lobbyists, and three editorials in Massachusetts newspapers constitute public opinion on a given issue. Yet in truth I rarely know how the great majority of the voters feel, or even how much they know of the issues that seem so burning in Washington.

Today the challenge of political courage looms larger than ever before. For our everyday life is becoming so saturated with the tremendous power of mass communications that any unpopular or unorthodox course arouses a storm of protests such as John Quincy Adams—under attack in 1807—could never have envisioned. Our political life is becoming so expensive, so mechanized and so dominated by professional politicians and public relations men that the idealist who dreams of independent statesmanship is rudely awakened by the necessities of election and accomplishment. And our public life is becoming so increasingly centered upon that seemingly unending war to which we have given the curious epithet "cold" that we tend to encourage rigid ideological unity and orthodox patterns of thought.

And thus, in the days ahead, only the very courageous will be able to take the hard and unpopular decisions necessary for our survival in the struggle with a powerful enemy—an enemy with leaders who need give little thought to the popularity of their course, who need pay little tribute to the public opinion they themselves manipulate, and who may force, without fear of retaliation at the polls, their citizens to sacrifice present laughter for future glory. And only the very courageous will be able to keep alive the spirit of individualism and dissent which gave birth to this nation, nourished it as an infant and carried it through its severest tests upon the attainment of its maturity.

Of course, it would be much easier if we could all continue to think in traditional political patterns—of liberalism and conservatism, as Republicans and Democrats, from the viewpoint of North and South, management and labor, business and consumer or some equally narrow framework. It would be more comfortable to continue to move and vote in platoons, joining whomever of our colleagues are equally enslaved by some current fashion, raging prejudice or popular movement. But today this nation cannot tolerate the luxury of such lazy political habits. Only the strength and progress and peaceful change that come from independent judgment and individual ideas—and even from the unorthodox and the eccentric—can enable us to surpass that foreign ideology that fears free thought more than it fears hydrogen bombs.

We shall need compromises in the days ahead, to be sure. But these will be, or should be, compromises of issues, not of principles. We can compromise our political positions, but not ourselves. We can resolve the clash of interests without conceding our ideals. And even the necessity for the right kind of compromise does not eliminate the need for those idealists and reformers who keep our compromises moving ahead, who prevent all political situations from meeting the description supplied by Shaw: "smirched with compromise, rotted with opportunism, mildewed by expedience, stretched out of shape with wirepulling and putrefied with permeation." Compromise need not mean cowardice. Indeed it is frequently the compromisers and conciliators who are faced with the severest tests of political courage as they oppose the extremist views of their constituents. It was because Daniel Webster conscientiously favored compromise in 1850 that he earned a condemnation unsurpassed in the annals of political history.

His is a story worth remembering today. So, I believe, are the stories of other Senators of courage—men whose abiding loyalty to their nation triumphed over all personal and political considerations, men who showed the real meaning of courage and a real faith in democracy, men who made the Senate of the United States something more than a mere collection of robots dutifully recording the views of their constituents, or a gathering of time-servers skilled only in predicting and following the tides of public sentiment.

Some of these men, whose stories follow, were right in their beliefs; others perhaps were not. Some were ultimately vindicated by a return to popularity; many were not. Some showed courage throughout the whole of their political lives; others sailed with the wind until the decisive moment when their conscience, and events, propelled them into the center of the storm. Some were courageous in their unyielding devotion to absolute principles; others were damned for advocating compromise.

Whatever their differences, the American politicians whose stories are here retold shared that one heroic quality—courage. In the pages that follow, I have attempted to set forth their lives—the ideals they lived for and the principles they fought for, their virtues and their sins, their dreams and their disillusionments, the praise they earned and the abuse they endured. All this may be set down on the printed page. It is ours to write about, it is ours to read about. But there was in the lives of each of these men something that it is difficult for the printed page to capture—and yet something that has reached the homes and enriched the heritage of every citizen in every part of the land.

PART ONE

The Time and the Place

As our first story begins, in 1803, Washington was no more than a raw, country village. Legend has it that a new French envoy, looking about upon his arrival, cried: "My God! What have I done to be condemned to reside in this city!" In the unfinished Capitol sat the Senate of the United States, already vastly different from that very first Senate which had sat in the old New York City Hall in 1789, and even more different from the body originally planned by the makers of the Constitution in 1787.

The founding fathers could not have envisioned service in the Senate as providing an opportunity for "political courage," whereby men would endanger or end their careers by resisting the will of their constituents. For their very concept of the Senate, in contrast to the House, was of a body which would not be subject to constituent pressures. Each state, regardless of size and population, was to have the same number of Senators, as though they were ambassadors from individual sovereign state governments to the Federal Government, not representatives of the voting public. Senators would not stand for re-election every two years—indeed, Alexander Hamilton suggested they be given life tenure—and a six-year term was intended to insulate them from public opinion.

Nor were Senators even to be elected by popular vote; the state legislatures, which could be relied upon to represent the conservative property interests of each state and to resist the "follies of the masses," were assigned that function. In this way, said Delegate John Dickinson to the Constitutional Convention, the Senate would "consist of the most distinguished characters, distinguished for their rank in life and their weight of property, and bearing as strong a likeness to the British House of Lords as possible."

Moreover, the Senate was to be less of a legislative body—where heated debates on vital issues would be followed anxiously by the public—and more of an executive council, passing on appointments and treaties and generally advising the President, without public galleries or even a journal of its own proceedings. Local prejudices, said Hamilton, were to be forgotten on the Senate floor, else it would simply be a repetition of the Continental Congress where "the first question has been 'how will such a measure affect my constituents and . . . my re-election.' "

The original twenty-two United States Senators, meeting in New York in 1789, at first seemed to fulfill the expectations of the makers of the Constitution, particularly regarding its resemblance to the House of Lords. A distinguished and glittering gathering of eminent and experienced statesmen, the Senate, as compared with the House of Representatives, was on the whole far more pompous and formal, its chambers far more elaborate, and its members far more concerned with elegance of dress and social rank. Meeting behind closed doors, without the use of standing committees, the Senate consulted personally with President Washington, and acted very nearly as an integral part of the administration.

But, as it must to all legislative bodies, politics came to the United States Senate. As the Federalist party split on foreign policy and Thomas Jefferson resigned from the Cabinet to organize his followers, the Senate became a forum for criticism of the executive branch, and the role of executive council was assumed instead by a Cabinet of men upon whom the President could depend to share his views and be responsible to him. Other precedents had already divided the Senate and the White House. In 1789 "Senatorial Courtesy" rejected Benjamin Fishbourne as officer of the Port of Savannah because he was unacceptable to the Georgia Senators. Shortly thereafter, special committees launched the first Senate investigations of Administration policies and practices. And in that same year the impossibility of the Senate's role as an executive council became apparent when a Northwest Indian Treaty was being discussed in person with the Senate by Washington and his Secretary of War. Senator Maclay and others, fearful (as he expressed it in his diary) that "the President wishes to tread on the necks of the Senate," sought to refer the matter to a select committee. The President, Maclay records,

> started up in a violent fret . . . [and withdrew] with a discontented air. Had it been any other man than the man whom I wish to regard as the first character in the world, I would have said with sullen dignity.

Gradually the Senate assumed more of the aspects of a legislative body. In 1794 public galleries were authorized for regular legislative sessions; in 1801 newspaper correspondents were admitted; and by 1803 the Senate was debating who should have the privilege of coming upon the Senate floor. Congressmen, Ambassadors, Department Heads and Governors could be agreed upon, but what about "the ladies"? Senator Wright contended "that their presence gives a pleasing and necessary animation to debate, polishing the speakers' arguments and softening their manner." But John Quincy Adams, whose puritanical candor on such occasions will be subsequently noted, replied that the ladies "introduced noise and confusion into the Senate, and debates were protracted to arrest their attention." (The motion to admit "the ladies" was defeated 16-12, although this policy of exclusion would be reversed in later years, only to be restored in modern times.)

Although Senators were paid the munificent sum of $6 per day, and their privileges included the use of great silver snuffboxes on the Senate floor, the aristocratic manners which had characterized the first Senate were strangely out of place when the struggling hamlet of Washington became the capital city in 1800, for its rugged surroundings contrasted sharply with those enjoyed at the temporary capitals in New York and Philadelphia. Formality in Senate procedures was retained, however—although Vice President Aaron Burr, himself an object of some disrepute after killing Hamilton in a duel, frequently found it necessary to call Senators to order for "eating apples and cakes in their seats" and walking between those engaged in discussion. And John Quincy Adams noted in his diary that some of his colleagues' speeches "were so wild and so bluntly expressed as to be explained only by recognizing that the member was inflamed by drink." But certainly the Senate retained greater dignity than the House, where Members might sit with hat on head and feet on desk, watching John Randolph of Roanoke stride in wearing silver spurs, carrying a heavy riding whip, followed by a foxhound which slept beneath his desk, and calling to the doorkeeper for more liquor as he launched vicious attacks upon his opponents.

Nevertheless, the House, still small enough to be a truly deliberative body, overshadowed the Senate in terms of political power during the first three decades of our government. Madison said that "being a young man and desirous of increasing his reputation as a statesman, he could not afford to accept a seat in the Senate," whose debates had little influence on public opinion. Many Senators surrendered their seats to become members of the House, or to hold other state and local offices; and the Senate frequently adjourned to permit its members to hear an important House debate.

Senator Maclay, whose diary provides the best, if somewhat acidly warped, record of that early Senate, frequently complained of dull and trivial sessions, as witness this entry for April 3, 1790: "Went to the Hall. The minutes were read. A message was received from the President of the United States. A report was handed to the Chair. We looked and laughed at each other for half an hour, and adjourned."

But as the Senate shed its role as executive council and entered on a more equal basis with the House into the legislative process, it also became apparent that no Constitutional safeguards, however nobly created, could prevent political and constituent pressures from entering those deliberations. Maclay was disgusted that, in place of "the most delicate honor, the most exalted wisdom and the most refined generosity" governing every act and deed of his colleagues, as he had expected, he found "the basest selfishness. . . . Our government is a mere system of jockeying opinions: 'Vote this way for me, and I will vote that way for you.' " The local prejudices which Hamilton had hoped to exclude only intensified, particularly as the Federalists of New England and the Jeffersonians of Virginia split along sectional as well as partisan lines. State legislatures, which would become increasingly responsive to those previously scorned "masses" as property qualifications for voting were removed, transmitted the political pressures of their own constituents to their Senators through "instructions" (a device which in this country apparently had originated in the old Puritan town meetings, which had instructed their deputies to the Massachusetts General Court on such measures as "removing the Capital from the wicked city of Boston," taking any steps possible "to exterminate the legal profession," and preventing debtors from paying their debts "with old rusty barrels of guns that are serviceable for no man, except to work up as old iron"). Some Senators were also required to return regularly to their state legislatures, to report like Venetian envoys on their stewardship at the Capital.

It was a time of change—in the Senate, in the concept of our government, in the growth of the two-party system, in the spread of democracy to the farm and the frontier and in the United States of America. Men who were flexible, men who could move with or ride over the changing currents of public opinion, men who sought their glory in the dignity of the Senate rather than its legislative accomplishments—these were the men for such times. But young John Quincy Adams of Massachusetts was not such a man.

II

JOHN QUINCY ADAMS

"The Magistrate Is the Servant Not . . . of the People, But of His God."

The young Senator from Massachusetts stirred restlessly in his chair as the debate droned on. The half-filled Senate chamber fairly echoed with the shouting of his Massachusetts colleague, Senator Pickering, who was denouncing President Jefferson's Trade Embargo of 1807 for what seemed like the one hundredth time. Outside, a dreary January rain had bogged the dismal village of Washington in a sea of mud. Sorting the mail from Massachusetts which lay in disarray on his desk, John Quincy Adams found his eye caught by an unfamiliar handwriting, on an envelope with no return address. Inside was a single sheet of fine linen paper, and the Senator grimly read its anonymous message a second time before crumpling letter and envelope into the basket by his desk:

Lucifer, Son of the Morning, how thou hast fallen! We hope not irrecoverably. Oh Adams, remember who thou art. Return to Massachusetts! Return to thy country. Assist not in its destruction! Consider the consequences! Awake—arouse in time!

A Federalist

A Federalist! Adams mused bitterly over the word. Was he not the son of the last Federalist President? Had he not served Federalist administrations in the diplomatic service abroad? Had he not been elected as a Federalist to the Massachusetts Legislature and then to the United States Senate? Now, simply because he had placed national interest before party and section, the Federalists had deserted him. Yes, he thought, I did not desert them, as they charged—it is they who have deserted me.

> My political prospects are declining [he wrote in his diary that night] and as my term of service draws near its close, I am constantly approaching to the certainty of being restored to the situation of a private citizen. For this event, however, I hope to have my mind sufficiently prepared. In the meantime, I implore that Spirit from whom every good and perfect gift descends to enable me to render essential service to my country, and that I may never be governed in my public conduct by any consideration other than that of my duty.

These are not merely the sentiments of a courageous Senator, they are also the words of a Puritan statesman. For John Quincy Adams was one of the great representatives of that extraordinary breed who have left a memorable imprint upon our Government and our way of life. Harsh and intractable, like the rocky New England countryside which colored his attitude toward the world at large, the Puritan gave meaning, consistency and character to the early days of the American Republic. His somber sense of responsibility toward his Creator he carried into every phase of his daily life. He believed that man was made in the image of God, and thus he believed him equal to the extraordinary demands of self-government. The Puritan loved liberty and he loved the law; he had a genius for determining the precise point where the rights of the state and the rights of the individual could be reconciled. The intellect of the Puritan—of John Quincy Adams and his forebears—was, as George Frisbie Hoar has said:

fit for exact ethical discussion, clear in seeing general truths, active, unresting, fond of inquiry and debate, but penetrated and restrained by a shrewd common sense. . . . He had a tenacity of purpose, a lofty and inflexible courage, an unbending will, which never qualified or flinched before human antagonist, or before exile, torture, or death.

In John Quincy Adams these very characteristics were unhappily out of tune with the party intrigues and political passions of the day. Long before those discouraging months in the Senate when his mail was filled with abuse from the Massachusetts Federalists, long before he had even entered the Senate, he had noted in his diary the dangers that confronted a Puritan entering politics: "I feel strong temptation to plunge into political controversy," he had written, "but . . . a politician in this country must be the man of a party. I would fain be the man of my whole country."

* * *

Abigail Adams had proudly told her friends when John Quincy was still a boy that she and her husband, who completely directed his education and training, had marked their son for future leadership "in the Cabinet or the field . . . a guardian of his country's laws and liberties." Few if any Americans have been born with the advantages of John Quincy Adams: a famous name; a brilliant father who labored unceasingly to develop his son's natural talents; and an extraordinary mother. Indeed he was born with everything to make for a happy and successful life except for those qualities that bring peace of mind. In spite of a life of extraordinary achievement, he was gnawed constantly by a sense of inadequacy, of frustration, of failure. Though his hard New England conscience and his remarkable talents drove him steadily along a road of unparalleled success, he had from the beginning an almost morbid sense of constant failure.

His early feelings of inadequacy, as well as his precocious mind, were evidenced by the letter he wrote his father at age nine:

Dear Sir:

I love to receive letters very well; much better than I love to write them. I make but a poor figure at composition. My head is much too fickle. My thoughts are running after bird's eggs, play and trifles, till I get vexed with myself. Mamma has a troublesome task to keep me a studying. I own I am ashamed of myself. I have but just entered the third volume of Rollin's History, but designed to have got half through it by this time. I am determined this week to be more diligent. I have set myself a stint to read the third volume half out. If I can but keep my resolution, I may again at the end of the week give a better account of myself. I wish, sir, you would give me in writing some instructions with regard to the use of my time, and advise me how to proportion my studies and play, and I will keep them by me, and endeavor to follow them.

With the present determination of growing better, I am, dear sir, your son,

JOHN QUINCY ADAMS

Again, thirty-six years later, having served as United States Senator, Harvard professor, and American Minister to major European powers, he could write sadly in his diary:

I am forty-five years old. Two-thirds of a long life have passed, and I have done nothing to distinguish it by usefulness to my country and to mankind. . . . Passions, indolence, weakness and infirmities have sometimes made me swerve from my better knowledge of right and almost constantly paralyzed my efforts of good.

And finally, at age seventy, having distinguished himself as a brilliant Secretary of State, an independent President and an eloquent member of Congress, he was to record somberly that his "whole life has been a succession of disappointments. I can scarcely recollect a single instance of success in anything that I ever undertook."

Yet the lifetime which was so bitterly deprecated by its own principal has never been paralleled in American history. John Quincy Adams—until his death at eighty in the Capitol—held more important offices and participated in more important events than anyone in the history of our nation, as Minister to the Hague, Emissary to England, Minister to Prussia, State Senator, United States Senator, Minister to Russia, Head of the American Mission to negotiate peace with England, Minister to England, Secretary of State, President of the United States and member of the House of Representatives. He figured, in one capacity or another, in the American Revolution, the War of 1812 and the prelude to the Civil War. Among the acquaintances and colleagues who march across the pages of his diary are Sam Adams (a kinsman), John Hancock, Washington, Jefferson, Franklin, Lafayette, John Jay, James Madison, James Monroe, John Marshall, Henry Clay, Andrew Jackson, Thomas Hart Benton, John Tyler, John C. Calhoun, Daniel Webster, Lincoln, James Buchanan, William Lloyd Garrison, Andrew Johnson, Jefferson Davis and many others.

Though one of the most talented men ever to serve his nation, he had few of the personal characteristics which ordinarily give color and charm to personality. But there is a fascination and nobility in this picture of a man unbending, narrow and intractable, judging himself more severely than his most bitter enemies judged him, possessing an integrity unsurpassed among the major political figures of our history, and constantly driven onward by his conscience and his deeply felt obligation to be worthy of his parents, their example and their precepts.

His frustrations and defeats in political office—as Senator and President—were the inevitable result of this intransigence in ignoring the political facts of life. It is significant to note that the two Adamses, father and son, were the only Presidents not elected for a second term in the first fifty years of our nation's history. Yet their failures, if they can be called failures, were the result of their own undeviating devotion to what they considered to be the public interest and the result of the inability of their contemporaries to match the high standards of honor and rectitude that they brought to public life.

The story of the son is not wholly separable from the story of the father. For John Quincy Adams was, as Samuel Eliot Morison has described him, "above all an Adams"; and his heartwarming devotion to his father and the latter's steadfast loyalty to his son regardless of political embarrassment offer a single ray of warmth in that otherwise hard, cold existence. ("What a queer family!" Federalist leader Harrison Otis wrote in later years. "I think them all varieties in a peculiar species of our race exhibiting a combination of talents and good moral character with passions and prejudices calculated to defeat their own objects and embarrass their friends.") As a child in a tightly knit Puritan family, John Quincy had been taught by his mother to emulate his famous father; and as a Senator, when colleagues and friends deserted him on every side, it was to his father that he turned for support and approval.

Even after the death of the elder Adams, John Quincy maintained touching loyalty to his father's memory. Reading in Jefferson's works the letters written by the latter more than thirty-five years earlier when his father and Jefferson had been political rivals (although their early friendship was later revived), he could still work himself into a rage at what he regarded as Jefferson's perfidy. "His treatment of my father," Adams wrote in his diary, "was double-dealing, treacherous and false beyond all toleration." John Quincy did not comprehend, after a lifetime in the thick of it, how our complicated Federal system of checks and balances operated; nor did he realize that what he regarded as Jefferson's "machinations" was merely a facet of the latter's genius applied with success to the art and science of Government.

The failure of John Quincy Adams to recognize the political facts of life first became apparent during his years in the Senate, years which were neither the most productive of his life nor those in which his contribution was especially significant. Yet his single term in the United States Senate gives us a clear insight into the fate of a man who brought to the public service notable faculties, a respected name and a singular ambition for the right. His experience illustrates as does almost none other that even this extraordinary equipment is not enough to succeed in American political life.

* * *

It was not unnatural that John Quincy, returning to Boston after diplomatic service abroad upon his father's defeat for President by Thomas Jefferson, should become active in the affairs of his father's party. He admired the Federalists as the founders of the Constitution, the champions of naval power and a bulwark against French Revolutionary influences.

But no sooner had the young ex-diplomat been elected as a Federalist to the Massachusetts Legislature when he demonstrated his audacious disdain for narrow partisanship. Without consulting his senior colleagues, he proposed—only forty-eight hours after he had become a member of that august legislative body—that the Republican (Jeffersonian or Democratic) party be given proportional representation on the Governor's council. (Adams later noted that this act of nonpartisan independence "marked the principle by which my whole public life has been governed from that day to this.")

In subsequently selecting young Adams for the Senate, his colleagues in the state legislature may have assumed that the honor for one of his comparative youth would help impress upon him his obligations to his party.

But while with one hand the legislature moved young John Quincy nearer his vision of service to the nation, with the other it rudely ripped through the fabric of his dream and placed real and unpleasant obstacles in his path. For upon the heels of his election, the jealous and antagonistic Timothy Pickering (who had been dismissed as Secretary of State by his father) was selected as Adams' Senatorial colleague to fill a short-term vacancy. Neither Pickering nor Adams entertained any illusions about the former's bitter enmity toward the entire Adams family, and John Quincy realized that as a well-known and powerful Federalist, Senator Pickering would be able to channel upon his young colleague all the dislikes and suspicions which the remaining Federalist Senators had harbored for the independence shown by the senior Adams as President. Nor could he expect sympathy from Jefferson's Republican Senators, who had recently completed a bitter campaign against his father and the Alien and Sedition Laws which bore his approval. Noting in his diary that "the qualities of mind most peculiarly called for are firmness, perseverance, patience, coolness and forbearance," John Quincy Adams, like any Puritan gentleman, set out for Washington determined to meet the standards of self-discipline which he had imposed upon himself.

Arriving in Washington, Adams promptly indicated his disregard for both party affiliations and customary freshman reticence. Although illness in the family had prevented him from arriving in time to vote on ratification of President Jefferson's treaty for the purchase of the Louisiana Territory, he promptly aroused a storm of controversy by becoming the only Federalist to support that precedent-shattering acquisition actively on the floor and to vote for an $11 million appropriation to effectuate it. His democratic principles also caused him to fight administration measures for imposing a government and taxes upon the residents of the Territory—

thus incurring the opposition of his Republican colleagues as well. But, with a vision of an America stretched to its continental limits, he regarded Jefferson's remarkable feat in excluding Napoleon from our boundaries while enriching our nation as far more important than the outraged astonishment of his Federalist colleagues. Concerned primarily with maintaining the hegemony of New England, they feared westward expansion would diminish the political and economic influence of the commercial cities of the Northeast, lower the value of Eastern lands in which they were financially interested, and provide the Jeffersonians with a permanent majority in Congress. The young Federalist from Massachusetts, as though he were oblivious to their attitude, heaped fuel upon the fires of Federalist rage by attending a banquet of Jeffersonians in celebration of the purchase!

"The dinner was bad and the toasts too numerous," Adams complained dourly in his diary that night. But it is doubtful that even a feast reminiscent of Boston's finest inns would have made his attendance worth while —for this was regarded by his Federalist friends as the final proof of perfidy.

"Curse on the stripling, how he apes his sire!" wrote Theodore Lyman, a prominent Federalist who had sided with Pickering in the latter's falling-out with the senior Adams. But there was only one Federalist politician whose opinion young John Quincy valued above his own —John Adams. Anxiously, he sought his father's views, and the reassurance he received from that elder statesman early in 1804 compensated for all the abuse he had received at the hands of his father's party. "I do not disapprove of your conduct in the business of Louisiana," John Adams wrote his son, "though I know it will become a very unpopular subject in the northern states. . . . I think you have been right!"

In his diary young Adams summed up his first months in the Senate:

> I have already had occasion to experience, which I had before the fullest reason to expect, the danger of adhering to my own principles. The country is so totally given up to the spirit of party that not to follow blindfolded the one or the other is an expiable offence. . . . Between both, I see the impossibility of pursuing the dictates of my own conscience without sacrificing every prospect, not merely of advancement, but even of retaining that character and reputation I have enjoyed. Yet my choice is made, and, if I cannot hope to give satisfaction to my country, I am at least determined to have the approbation of my own reflections.

The possession of the proud name of Adams could not prevent—and may well have hastened—the young Senator's gradual emergence as a minority of one. Had his political philosophy been more popular, his personal mannerisms would still have made close alliances difficult. He was, after all, "an Adams . . . cold, tactless and rigidly conscientious." The son of an unpopular father, a renegade in his party and rather brash for a freshman Senator, John Quincy neither sought nor was offered political alliances or influence.

After only ten days in the Senate he had irritated his seniors and precipitated a three-hour debate by objecting to a routine resolution calling upon Senators to wear crepe one month in honor of three recently deceased patriots. Such a resolution, he somewhat impertinently argued, was improper if not unconstitutional by "tending to unsuitable discussions of character, and to debates altogether foreign to the subjects which properly belong" in the Senate. Next he astounded his colleagues by seeking to disqualify from an impeachment hearing any Senator who had previously voted on the impeachment resolution as a Member of the House. Then to show his stubborn intellectual independence, he alone opposed a motion to go into executive session when its sole purpose, he thought, was to give in the *Journal* an appearance of doing business when actually there was none to be done.

But if the Federalist party learned to dislike the "stripling" even more intensely than they had disliked "his sire," it must be said that any Federalist love for John Quincy would have been wasted anyway. For he became increasingly contemptuous of the Federalist party. An American nationalist who had lived a great part of his brief life abroad, he could not yield his devotion to the national interest for the narrowly partisan, parochial and pro-British outlook which dominated New England's first political party. His former colleagues in the State Legislature publicly charged him with ungrateful "conduct worthy of Machiavelli"; but he wrote his mother that he felt that, as Senator, he could best determine what Massachusetts' best interests were, and "if Federalism consists in looking to the British navy as the only palladium of our liberty, I must be a political heretic."

Many Senators before and after 1804 have combatted the ill-effects of being termed a political heretic by their party chieftains by building strong personal popularity among their constituents. This became increasingly possible as universal manhood suffrage became general early in the nineteenth century. But not John Quincy Adams. He regarded every public measure that came before him, a fellow Senator observed, as though it were an abstract proposition from Euclid, unfettered by considerations of political appeal. He denied the duty of elected representatives "to be palsied by the will of their constituents"; and he refused to achieve success by becoming what he termed a "patriot by profession," by pretending "extraordinary solicitude for the people, by flattering their prejudices, by ministering to their passions, and by humoring their transient and changeable opinions." His guiding star was the principle of Puritan statesmanship his father had laid down many years before: *"The magistrate is the servant not of his own desires, not even of the people, but of his God."*

We would admire the courage and determination of John Quincy Adams if he served in the Senate today. We would respect his nonpartisan, nonsectional approach. But I am not so certain that we would like him as a person; and it is apparent that many of his colleagues, on both sides of the aisle, did not. His isolation from either political party, and the antagonisms which he aroused, practically nullified the impact of his own independent and scholarly propositions. His diary reveals that the young Senator was not wholly insensitive to his increasing political isolation: he complained that he had "nothing to do but to make fruitless opposition." "I have already seen enough to ascertain that no amendments of my proposing will obtain in the Senate as now filled." "I have no doubt of incurring much censure and obloquy for this measure." And he referred to those "who hate me rather more than they love any principle." He was particularly bitter about Pickering's contemptuous conduct toward him, and felt that his colleague "abandons altogether the ground of right, and relies upon what is expedient."

But it was not until 1807 that the split between party and Senator became irreparable, and Adams was denounced by the great majority of his constituents, as well as the party chiefs. The final break, naturally enough, concerned this nation's foreign policy. As our relations with Great Britain worsened, our ships were seized, our cargoes were confiscated, and our seamen were "impressed" by British cruisers and compelled to serve—as alleged British subjects—in the King's navy. Thousands of American seamen were taken on an organized basis, ships were lost at sea for want of men, and even those able to "prove" American citizenship were frequently refused permission to return. Adams' patriotic instincts were aroused, and he was indignant that the very Federalist merchants whose ships were attacked had decided that appeasement of Great Britain was the only answer to their problems. His Federalist colleagues even attempted to rationalize such aggressive measures by talking vaguely of Britain's difficulties in her war with France and our friendly tone toward the latter. With undisguised contempt for this attitude, Adams in 1806 had introduced and pushed to passage—successfully—a unique experience for him, he noted in his diary—a series of resolutions condemning British aggressions upon American ships, and requesting the President to demand restoration and indemnification of the confiscated vessels. The Federalists, of course, had solidly opposed his measures, as they did an Adams-supported administration bill limiting British imports. He was now, for all practical purposes, a man without a party.

Finally, in the summer of 1807, the American frigate *Chesapeake* was summarily fired upon off the Virginia Capes by the British man-of-war *Leopard,* after the American vessel had refused either to be searched or to hand over four seamen whom the English claimed to be British subjects. Several of the American crew were killed or injured. The incensed Adams was convinced that, party or no party, the time for forceful action against such intolerable acts had come. He pleaded with local Federalist officials to call a town meeting in Boston to protest the incident. Turned down, and outraged when a prominent Federalist attempted to justify even the *Leopard's* attack, he discovered to his grim satisfaction that the Republican party was organizing a similar mass meeting to be held at the State House that very week.

The Federalist *Repertory* warned the faithful that the meeting represented nothing but an "irregular and tumultuous mode of proceeding," which "no just or honorable man" should attend. But John Quincy Adams did attend; and, although he declined to serve as moderator, he nevertheless was instrumental in drafting the group's fighting resolution which pledged to the President the lives and fortunes of the participants in support of "any measures, however serious."

Now the Federalists were outraged. Although they hurriedly called an official town meeting to pledge hypocritically their support to the President too, they stated publicly that John Quincy Adams, for his public association with Republican meetings and causes, should "have his head taken off for apostasy . . . and should no longer be considered as having any communion with the party." It was this episode, the Senator later commented, "which alienated me from that day and forever from the councils of the Federalist party."

When Jefferson on September 18, 1807, called upon Congress to retaliate against the British by enacting an embargo effectively shutting off all further international trade—a measure apparently ruinous to Massachusetts, the leading commercial state in the nation—it was John Quincy Adams of Massachusetts who rose on the Senate floor and called for referral of the message to a select committee; who was appointed Chairman of the committee; and who reported both the Embargo Bill and a bill of his own preventing British vessels from entering American waters.

"This measure will cost you and me our seats," young Adams remarked to a colleague, as the select committee completed its work and its members made their way to the Senate floor, "but private interest must not be put in opposition to public good."

His words were unerringly prophetic. As the Embargo Bill, with his help, became law, a storm of protest arose in Massachusetts reminiscent of the days of the Boston Tea Party. In that state were located a substantial proportion of America's merchant fleet and practically all of the shipbuilding and fishing industries. The embargo completely idled the shipbuilding industry, destroyed the shipping trade and tied up the fishing vessels; and stagnation, bankruptcy, distress, and migration from the territory became common. Neither merchants nor seamen could be convinced that the act was for their own good. Even the farmers of New England found their products a glut on the market, their export outlets having been closed.

The Federalist leaders insisted the Embargo was an attempt by Jefferson to ruin New England prosperity, to provoke England to war, and to aid the French. Even though New England Republicans refused to defend their President's bill, the Federalist party, scoring heavily on the issue, returned triumphantly to power in both Houses of the Massachusetts legislature. Talk of New England seceding became commonplace.

But however great their hatred for Jefferson and his Embargo, Massachusetts Federalists, merchants and other citizens were even more bitter over the "desertion" of their Senator to the ranks of the enemy. "A party scavenger!" snorted the Northampton *Hampshire Gazette*, "one of those ambitious politicians who lives on both land and water, and occasionally resorts to each, but who finally settles down in the mud." Adams, said the Salem *Gazette*, is "a popularity seeker . . . courting the prevailing party," and one of "Bonaparte's Senators." The Greenfield *Gazette* called him an apostate "associated with the assassins of his father's character." His own social circles in Boston—the rich, the cultivated and the influential—all turned against him. "I would not sit at the same table with that renegade," retorted one of Boston's leading citizens in refusing to attend a dinner at which Adams would be present. And a leading Federalist wrote with glee to the Washington party stalwarts, "He walks into State Street at the usual hour but seems totally unknown."

John Quincy Adams was alone—but not quite alone. "Most completely was I deserted by my friends, in Boston and in the state legislature," he wrote his mother. "I can never be sufficiently grateful to Providence that my father and my mother did not join in this general desertion." For when the unmerciful abuse from his home state was first heaped upon him, John Quincy had again turned to his father and poured out his feelings. And his father replied that his son's situation was "clear, plain and obvious":

> You are supported by no party; you have too honest a heart, too independent a mind, and too brilliant talents, to be sincerely and confidentially trusted by any man who is under the domination of party maxims or party feelings. . . . You may depend upon it then that your fate is decided. . . . You ought to know and expect this and by no means regret it. My advice to you is steadily to pursue the course you are in, with moderation and caution however, because I think it the path of justice.

But the entire Adams family was damned in the eyes of the ex-President's former supporters by his son's act of courage. "His [John Quincy's] apostasy is no longer a matter of doubt with anybody," cried Representative Gardenier of New York. "I wish to God that the noble house of Braintree had been put in a hole—and a deep one, too—20 years ago!" But father and son, the Adamses stood together. "Parton has denounced you as No Federalist," his father wrote, "and I wish he would denounce me in the same manner, for I have long since renounced, abdicated, and disclaimed the name and character and attributes of that sect, as it now appears."

With his father's support—in a fight where he stood with the President who had defeated his father!—John Quincy maintained the unflinching and inflexible bearing which became his Puritan ancestry. When he was accosted in Boston by a politically minded preacher who assailed his views "in a rude and indecent manner, I told him that in consideration of his age I should only remark that he had one lesson yet to learn—Christian charity."

When his colleague Pickering denounced him in an open letter to the Legislature which was distributed throughout Massachusetts in tens of thousands, he wrote a masterful reply—criticizing the Federalist party as sectional, outmoded and unpatriotic; insisting that the critical issues of war and peace could not be decided on the basis of "geographical position, party bias or professional occupation"; and exploding at Pickering's servile statement that "Although Great Britain, with her thousand ships of war, could have destroyed our commerce, she has really done it no essential injury."

The Federalist Legislature convened at the end of May 1808, with as the Massachusetts Republican Governor wrote Jefferson—but one "principal object—the political and even the personal destruction of John Quincy Adams." As soon as both Houses had organized, the legislature immediately elected Adams' successor—nine months prior to the expiration of his term! And as its next order of business, the Legislature promptly passed resolutions instructing its Senators to urge repeal of the Embargo.

"The election," Adams realized, "was precipitated for the sole purpose of specially marking me. For it ought, in regular order, not to have been made until the winter session of the legislature." And the resolutions, he felt, enjoined "upon their Senators a course of conduct which neither my judgment could approve nor my spirit brook."

Only one course was conscientiously open to him—he resigned his seat in the Senate in order to defend the policies of the man who had driven his father from the Presidency.

It was "out of the question," he wrote, to hold his seat "without exercising the most perfect freedom of agency, under the sole and exclusive control of my own sense of right."

> I will only add, that, far from regretting any one of those acts for which I have suffered, I would do them over again,

were they now to be done, at the hazard of ten times as much slander, unpopularity, and displacement.

But had his own vote in the Senate been necessary to save Jefferson's foreign policy, Adams wrote to those who criticized his departure at such a critical time, then "highly as I reverenced the authority of my constituents, and bitter as would have been the cup of resistance to their declared will . . . I would have defended their interests against their inclinations, and incurred every possible addition to their resentment, to save them from the vassalage of their own delusions."

Hated by the Federalists and suspected by the Republicans, John Quincy Adams returned to private life. His star was soon to rise again; but he never forgot this incident or abandoned his courage of conscience. (Legend has it that during Adams' politically independent term as President, in response to the Presidential toast "May he strike confusion to his foes!" Daniel Webster dryly commented, "As he has already done to his friends.") Soon after his retirement from the White House in 1829, Adams was asked by the voters of the Plymouth District to represent them in Congress. In disregard of the advice of his family and friends and his own desire for leisure time to write his father's biography, he agreed to accept the post if elected. But he specified, first, that he should never be expected to promote himself as a candidate and ask for votes; and, secondly, that he would pursue a course in Congress completely independent of the party and people who elected him. On this basis Adams was elected by an overwhelming vote, and served in the House until his death. Here he wrote perhaps the brightest chapter of his history, for as "Old Man Eloquent" he devoted his remarkable prestige and tireless energies to the struggle against slavery.

To be returned on this independent basis to the Congress from which he had departed so ignominiously twenty-two years earlier was a deeply moving experience for the courageous ex-Senator. "I am a member-elect of the Twenty-Second Congress," he recorded with pride in his diary. "No election or appointment conferred upon me ever gave me so much pleasure. My election as President of the United States was not half so gratifying to my inmost soul."

PART TWO

The Time and the Place

Great crises produce great men, and great deeds of courage. This country has known no greater crisis than that which culminated in the fratricidal war between North and South in 1861. Thus, without intending to slight other periods of American history, no work of this nature could overlook three acts of outstanding political courage—of vital importance to the eventual maintenance of the Union—which occurred in the fateful decade before the Civil War. In two cases—involving Senators Sam Houston of Texas and Thomas Hart Benton of Missouri, both of whom had enjoyed political dominion in their states for many years—defeat was their reward. In the third—that involving Daniel Webster of Massachusetts—even death, which came within two years of his great decision, did not halt the calumnies heaped upon him by his enemies, who had sadly embittered his last days.

It is not surprising that this ten-year period of recurring crises, when the ties that bound the Union were successively snapping, should have brought forth the best, as it did the worst, in our political leaders. All in a position of responsibility were obliged to decide between maintaining their loyalty to the nation or to their state and region. For many on both sides—the abolitionists in the North, the fire-eaters in the South, men who were wholly convinced of the rightness of their section's cause—the decision came easily.

But to those who felt a dual loyalty to their state and their country, to those who sought compromises which would postpone or remove entirely the shadow of war which hung over them, the decision was agonizing, for the ultimate choice involved the breaking of old loyalties and friendships, and the prospect of humiliating political defeat.

The cockpit in which this struggle between North and South was fought was the chamber of the United States Senate. The South, faced with the steadily growing population of the North as reflected in increasing majorities in the House of Representatives, realized that its sole hope of maintaining its power and prestige lay in the Senate. It was for this reason that the admission of new states into the Union, which threatened continuously to upset the precarious balance of power between the free and the slave states, between the agricultural and manufacturing regions, was at the heart of some of the great Senate debates in the first half of the nineteenth century.

In 1820 a law was passed to admit Maine and Missouri into the Union together, one free, the other slave, as part of Henry Clay's first great compromise. In 1836 and 1837, Arkansas and Michigan, and in 1845 and 1846, Florida and Iowa, were admitted through legislation which coupled them together. But the seams of compromise were bursting by 1850, as vast new territories acquired by the Mexican War accelerated the pace of the slavery controversy. The attention of the nation was focused on the Senate, and focused especially on the three most gifted parliamentary leaders in American history—Clay, Calhoun and Webster. Of these, only Daniel Webster was to share with Benton and Houston the ignominy of constituent wrath and the humiliation of political downfall at the hands of the states they had loved and championed. We shall note well the courage of Webster, Benton and Houston; but if we are to understand the times that made their feats heroic, we must first note the leadership of the two Senate giants who formed with Webster the most outstanding triumvirate the Senate has ever known, Henry Clay and John C. Calhoun.

Henry Clay of Kentucky—bold, autocratic and magnetic, fiery in manner with a charm so compelling that an opponent once declined a meeting which would subject him to the appeal of Harry of the West. To Abraham Lincoln, "He was my beau ideal"; to the half-mad, half-genius John Randolph of Roanoke, he was, in what is perhaps the most memorable and malignant sentence in the history of personal abuse, "a being, so brilliant yet so corrupt, which, like a rotten mackerel by moonlight, shines and stinks." Not even John Calhoun, who had fought him for years, was impervious to his fascination: "I don't like Henry Clay. He is a bad man, an impostor, a creator of wicked schemes. I wouldn't speak to him, but, by God, I love him."

Others besides John Calhoun loved him. Like Charles James Fox, he reveled in a love for life, and had a matchless gift for winning and holding the hearts of his fellow-countrymen—and women. Elected to the Senate when still below the constitutional age of thirty, he was subsequently sent to the House, where in a move never duplicated before or since he was immediately elected Speaker at the age of thirty-five.

Though he lacked the intellectual resources of Webster and Calhoun, Henry Clay nevertheless had visions of a greater America beyond those held by either of his famous colleagues. And so, in 1820, 1833 and 1850 he initiated, hammered and charmed through reluctant Congresses the three great compromises that preserved the Union until 1861, by which time the strength of the North was such that secession was doomed to failure.

The second and probably the móst extraordinary of the triumvirate was John C. Calhoun of South Carolina, with bristling hair and eyes that burned like heavy coals, "the cast-iron man," according to the English spinster, Harriet Martineau, "who looks as if he had never been born, and never could be extinguished." Calhoun, in spite of this appearance, had been born—in 1782, the same year as Webster and five years after Clay. He was six feet, two inches tall; a graduate of Yale University; a Member of Congress at the age of twenty-nine; a War Hawk who joined Henry Clay in driving the United States into the War of 1812; a nationalist who turned sectionalist in the 1820's as the economic pressures of the tariff began to tell on the agricultural economy of South Carolina. Calhoun had a mind that was cold, narrow, concentrated and powerful. Webster considered him "much the ablest man in the Senate," the greatest in fact that he had met in his entire public life. "He could have," he declared, "demolished Newton, Calvin or even John Locke as a logician."

His speeches, stripped of all excess verbiage, marched across the Senate floor in even columns, measured, disciplined, carrying all before them. Strangely enough, although he had the appearance, especially in his later days, of a fanatic, he was a man of infinite charm and personality. He was reputed to be the best conversationalist in South Carolina, and he won to him through their emotions men who failed to comprehend his closely reasoned arguments. His hold upon the imagination and affection of the entire South steadily grew, and at his death in the midst of the great debate of 1850 he was universally mourned.

Calhoun believed that the Constitutional Convention

had not nationalized our government; that the sovereign states still retained "the right of judging . . . when the Congress encroached upon the individual state's power and liberty."

With other Southerners, he believed that the geography and climate of the Western country made it unlikely that slavery could ever prosper in many of the territories that were seeking to become states, and that only in the Southwest could they hope to balance the surging tide of free Western states by securing new slave states and Senators from the lands seized from Mexico. The Clay Compromise of 1850, which sought to conciliate the differences between North and South as to the ultimate fate of these lands, thus assumed far-reaching importance.

All of the currents of conflict and disunion, of growth and decline, of strength and weakness, came to a climax in 1850.

The three chief protagonists in the Washington drama of 1850 had been colleagues in Congress as far back as 1813. Then they were young, full of pride and passion and hope, and the world lay waiting before them. Now, nearly forty years later in the sunset of their lives—for they would all be dead within two years—with youth and illusions gone, they moved once again to the center of the stage.

But they were not alone in the struggle. Neither Senator Thomas Hart Benton nor Sam Houston was dwarfed by the towering reputations of his three colleagues. Each was a legend in his own lifetime—and occupying respectively the strategic border states of Missouri and Texas, it was inevitable that the choice that each would make as the country slowly drifted apart would affect the nature and outcome of the general struggle.

That secession did not occur in 1850 instead of 1861 is due in great part to Daniel Webster, who was in large measure responsible for the country's acceptance of

Henry Clay's compromise. The reasons he supported the compromise, the effect of his support and the calumnies he suffered are detailed in Chapter III.

That the key border state of Missouri did not join the Confederacy in 1861 was due in good measure to the memory of its former Senator Thomas Hart Benton. No man gave more than Senator Benton for the preservation of the Union. His efforts and his fate are told in Chapter IV.

Texas joined the Confederacy, but not without a struggle that made Senator Houston's old age a shipwreck. His story is told in Chapter V.

III

DANIEL WEBSTER

". . . Not as a Massachusetts Man . . . But as an American . . ."

The blizzardy night of January 21, 1850, was no night in Washington for an ailing old man to be out. But wheezing and coughing fitfully, Henry Clay made his way through the snowdrifts to the home of Daniel Webster. He had a plan—a plan to save the Union—and he knew he must have the support of the North's most renowned orator and statesman. He knew that he had no time to lose, for that very afternoon President Taylor, in a message to Congress asking California's admission as a free state, had only thrown fuel on the raging fire that threatened to consume the Union. Why had the President failed to mention New Mexico, asked the North? What about the Fugitive Slave Law being enforced, said the South? What about the District of Columbia slave trade, Utah, Texas boundaries? Tempers mounted, plots unfolded, disunity was abroad in the land.

But Henry Clay had a plan—a plan for another Great Compromise to preserve the nation. For an hour he outlined its contents to Daniel Webster in the warmth of the latter's comfortable home, and together they talked of saving the Union. Few meetings in American history have ever been so productive or so ironic in their consequences. For the Compromise of 1850 added to Henry Clay's garlands as the great Pacificator; but Daniel Webster's support which insured its success resulted in his political crucifixion, and, for half a century or more, his historical condemnation.

The man upon whom Henry Clay called that wintry night was one of the most extraordinary figures in American political history. Daniel Webster is familiar to many of us today as the battler for Jabez Stone's soul against the devil in Stephen Vincent Benét's story. But in his own lifetime, he had many battles against the devil for his own soul—and some he lost. Webster, wrote one of his intimate friends, was "a compound of strength and weakness, dust and divinity," or in Emerson's words "a great man with a small ambition."

There could be no mistaking he was a great man—he looked like one, talked like one, was treated like one and insisted he was one. With all his faults and failings, Daniel Webster was undoubtedly the most talented figure in our Congressional history: not in his ability to win men to a cause—he was no match in that with Henry Clay; not in his ability to hammer out a philosophy of government—Calhoun outshone him there; but in his ability to make alive and supreme the latent sense of oneness, of Union, that all Americans felt but which few could express.

But how Daniel Webster could express it! How he could express almost any sentiments! Ever since his first speech in Congress—attacking the War of 1812—had riveted the attention of the House of Representatives as no freshman had ever held it before, he was the outstanding orator of his day—indeed, of all time—in Congress, before hushed throngs in Massachusetts and as an advocate before the Supreme Court. Stern Chief Justice Marshall was said to have been visibly moved by

Webster's famous defense in the Dartmouth College case —"It is, sir, as I have said, a small college—and yet there are those who love it." After his oration on the two hundredth founding of Plymouth Colony, a young Harvard scholar wrote:

> I was never so excited by public speaking before in my life. Three or four times I thought my temple would burst with the rush of blood. . . . I was beside myself and I am still so.

And the peroration of his reply to Senator Hayne of South Carolina, when secession had threatened twenty years earlier, was a national rallying cry memorized by every schoolboy—"Liberty and Union, now and forever, one and inseparable!"

A very slow speaker, hardly averaging a hundred words a minute, Webster combined the musical charm of his deep organ-like voice, a vivid imagination, an ability to crush his opponents with a barrage of facts, a confident and deliberate manner of speaking and a striking appearance to make his orations a magnet that drew crowds hurrying to the Senate chamber. He prepared his speeches with the utmost care, but seldom wrote them out in a prepared text. It has been said that he could think out a speech sentence by sentence, correct the sentences in his mind without the use of a pencil and then deliver it exactly as he thought it out.

Certainly that striking appearance was half the secret of his power, and convinced all who looked upon his face that he was one born to rule men. Although less than six feet tall, Webster's slender frame when contrasted with the magnificent sweep of his shoulders gave him a theatrical but formidable presence. But it was his extraordinary head that contemporaries found so memorable, with the features Carlyle described for all to remember: "The tanned complexion, the amorphous crag-like face; the dull black eyes under the precipice of brows, like dull anthracite furnaces needing only to be blown; the mastiff mouth accurately closed." One contemporary called Webster "a living lie, because no man on earth could be so great as he looked."

And Daniel Webster was not as great as he looked. The flaw in the granite was the failure of his moral senses to develop as acutely as his other faculties. He could see nothing improper in writing to the President of the Bank of the United States—at the very time when the Senate was engaged in debate over a renewal of the Bank's charter—noting that "my retainer has not been received or refreshed as usual." But Webster accepted favors not as gifts but as services which he believed were rightly due him. When he tried to resign from the Senate in 1836 to recoup speculative losses through his law practice, his Massachusetts businessmen friends joined to pay his debts to retain him in office. Even at his deathbed, legend tells us, there was a knock at his door, and a large roll of bills was thrust in by an old gentleman, who said that "At such a time as this, there should be no shortage of money in the house."

Webster took it all and more. What is difficult to comprehend is that he saw no wrong in it—morally or otherwise. He probably believed that he was greatly underpaid, and it never occurred to him that by his own free choice he had sold his services and his talents, however extraordinary they might have been, to the people of the United States, and no one else, when he drew his salary as United States Senator. But Webster's support of the business interests of New England was not the result of the money he obtained, but of his personal convictions. Money meant little to him except as a means to gratify his peculiar tastes. He never accumulated a fortune. He never was out of debt. And he never was troubled by his debtor status. Sometimes he paid, and he always did so when it was convenient, but as Gerald W. Johnson says, "Unfortunately he sometimes paid in the wrong coin—not in legal tender—but in the confidence that the people reposed in him."

But whatever his faults, Daniel Webster remained the greatest orator of his day, the leading member of the American Bar, one of the most renowned leaders of the Whig party, and the only Senator capable of checking Calhoun. And thus Henry Clay knew he must enlist these extraordinary talents on behalf of his Great Compromise. Time and events proved he was right.

As the God-like Daniel listened in thoughtful silence, the sickly Clay unfolded his last great effort to hold the Union together. Its key features were five in number: (1) California was to be admitted as a free (nonslaveholding) state; (2) New Mexico and Utah were to be organized as territories without legislation either for or against slavery, thus running directly contrary to the hotly debated Wilmot Proviso which was intended to prohibit slavery in the new territories; (3) Texas was to be compensated for some territory to be ceded to New Mexico; (4) the slave trade would be abolished in the District of Columbia; and (5) a more stringent and enforceable Fugitive Slave Law was to be enacted to guarantee return to their masters of runaway slaves captured in Northern states. The Compromise would be condemned by the Southern extremists as appeasement, chiefly on its first and fourth provisions; and by the Northern abolitionists as 90 per cent concessions to the South with a meaningless 10 per cent sop thrown to the North, particularly because of the second and fifth provisions. Few Northerners could stomach any strengthening of the Fugitive Slave Act, the most bitterly hated measure—and until Prohibition, the most flagrantly disobeyed—ever passed by Congress. Massachusetts had even enacted a law making it a crime for anyone to enforce the provisions of the Act in that state!

How could Henry Clay then hope to win approval to such a plan from Daniel Webster of Massachusetts? Was he not specifically on record as a consistent foe of slavery and a supporter of the Wilmot Proviso? Had he not told the Senate in the Oregon Debate:

> I shall oppose all slavery extension and all increase of slave representation in all places, at all times, under all circumstances, even against all inducements, against all supposed limitation of great interests, against all combinations, against all compromises.

That very week he had written a friend: "From my earliest youth, I have regarded slavery as a great moral and political evil. . . . You need not fear that I shall vote for any compromise or do anything inconsistent with the past."

But Daniel Webster feared that civil violence "would only rivet the chains of slavery the more strongly." And the preservation of the Union was far dearer to his heart than his opposition to slavery.

And thus on that fateful January night, Daniel Webster promised Henry Clay his conditional support, and took inventory of the crisis about him. At first he shared the views of those critics and historians who scoffed at the possibility of secession in 1850. But as he talked with Southern leaders and observed "the condition of the country, I thought the inevitable consequences of leaving the existing controversies unadjusted would be Civil War." "I am nearly broken down with labor and anxiety," he wrote his son. "I know not how to meet the present emergency, or with what weapons to beat down the Northern and Southern follies now raging in equal extremes. . . . I have poor spirits and little courage."

Two groups were threatening in 1850 to break away from the United States of America. In New England, Garrison was publicly proclaiming, "I am an Abolitionist and, therefore, for the dissolution of the Union." And a mass meeting of Northern Abolitionists declared that "the Constitution is a covenant with death and an agreement with hell." In the South, Calhoun was writing to a friend in February of 1850, "Disunion is the only alternative that is left for us." And in his last great address to the Senate, read for him on March 4, only a few short weeks before his death, while he sat by too feeble to speak, he declared, "The South will be forced to choose between abolition and secession."

A preliminary convention of Southerners, also instigated by Calhoun, urged a full-scale convention of the South at Nashville for June of that fateful year to popularize the idea of dissolution.

The time was ripe for secession, and few were prepared to speak for union. Even Alexander Stephens of Georgia, anxious to preserve the Union, wrote friends in the South who were sympathetic with his views that "the feeling among the Southern members for a dissolution of the Union . . . is becoming much more general. Men are now beginning to talk of it seriously who twelve months ago hardly permitted themselves to think of it. . . . the crisis is not far ahead. . . . A dismemberment of this Republic I now consider inevitable." During the critical month preceding Webster's speech, six Southern states, each to secede ten years later, approved the aims of the Nashville Convention and appointed delegates. Horace Greeley wrote on February 23:

> There are sixty members of Congress who this day desire and are plotting to effect the idea of a dissolution of the Union. We have no doubt the Nashville Convention will be held and that the leading purpose of its authors is the separation of the slave states . . . with the formation of an independent confederacy.

Such was the perilous state of the nation in the early months of 1850.

By the end of February, the Senator from Massachusetts had determined upon his course. Only the Clay Compromise, Daniel Webster decided, could avert secession and civil war; and he wrote a friend that he planned "to make an honest truth-telling speech and a

Union speech, and discharge a clear conscience." As he set to work preparing his notes, he received abundant warning of the attacks his message would provoke. His constituents and Massachusetts newspapers admonished him strongly not to waver in his consistent anti-slavery stand, and many urged him to employ still tougher tones against the South. But the Senator from Massachusetts had made up his mind, as he told his friends on March 6, "to push my skiff from the shore alone." He would act according to the creed with which he had challenged the Senate several years earlier:

> Inconsistencies of opinion arising from changes of circumstances are often justifiable. But there is one sort of inconsistency that is culpable: it is the inconsistency between a man's conviction and his vote, between his conscience and his conduct. No man shall ever charge me with an inconsistency of that kind.

And so came the 7th of March, 1850, the only day in history which would become the title of a speech delivered on the Senate floor. No one recalls today—no one even recalled in 1851—the formal title Webster gave his address, for it had become the "Seventh of March" speech as much as Independence Day is known as the Fourth of July.

Realizing after months of insomnia that this might be the last great effort his health would permit, Webster stimulated his strength for the speech by oxide of arsenic and other drugs, and devoted the morning to polishing up his notes. He was excitedly interrupted by the Sergeant at Arms, who told him that even then—two hours before the Senate was to meet—the chamber, the galleries, the anterooms and even the corridors of the Capitol were filled with those who had been traveling for days from all parts of the nation to hear Daniel Webster. Many foreign diplomats and most of the House of Representatives were among those vying for standing room. As the Senate met, members could scarcely walk to their seats through the crowd of spectators and temporary seats made of public documents stacked on top of each other. Most Senators gave up their seats to ladies, and stood in the aisles awaiting Webster's opening blast.

As the Vice President's gavel commenced the session, Senator Walker of Wisconsin, who held the floor to finish a speech begun the day before, told the Chair that "this vast audience has not come to hear me, and there is but one man who can assemble such an audience. They expect to hear him, and I feel it is my duty, as it is my pleasure, to give the floor to the Senator from Massachusetts."

The crowd fell silent as Daniel Webster rose slowly to his feet, all the impressive powers of his extraordinary physical appearance—the great, dark, brooding eyes, the wonderfully bronzed complexion, the majestic domed forehead—commanding the same awe they had commanded for more than thirty years. Garbed in his familiar blue tailed coat with brass buttons, and a buff waistcoat and breeches, he deliberately paused a moment as he gazed about at the greatest assemblage of Senators ever to gather in that chamber—Clay, Benton, Houston, Jefferson Davis, Hale, Bell, Cass, Seward, Chase, Stephen A. Douglas and others. But one face was missing—that of the ailing John C. Calhoun.

All eyes were fixed on the speaker; no spectator save his own son knew what he would say. "I have never before," wrote a newspaper correspondent, "witnessed an occasion on which there was deeper feeling enlisted or more universal anxiety to catch the most distinct echo of the speaker's voice."

In his moments of magnificent inspiration, as Emerson once described him, Webster was truly "the great cannon loaded to the lips." Summoning for the last time that spell-binding oratorical ability, he abandoned his previous opposition to slavery in the territories, abandoned his constituents' abhorrence of the Fugitive Slave Law, abandoned his own place in the history and hearts of his countrymen and abandoned his last chance for the goal that had eluded him for over twenty years—the Presidency. Daniel Webster preferred to risk his career and his reputation rather than risk the Union.

"Mr. President," he began, "I wish to speak today, not as a Massachusetts man, nor as a Northern man, but as an American and a Member of the Senate of the United States. . . . I speak today for the preservation of the Union. Hear me for my cause."

He had spoken but for a short time when the gaunt, bent form of Calhoun, wrapped in a black cloak, was dramatically assisted into his seat, where he sat trembling, scarcely able to move, and unnoticed by the speaker. After several expressions of regret by Webster that illness prevented the distinguished Senator from South Carolina from being present, Calhoun struggled up, grasping the arms of his chair, and in a clear and ghostly voice proudly announced, "The Senator from South Carolina *is* in his seat." Webster was touched, and with tears in his eyes he extended a bow toward Calhoun, who sank back exhausted and feeble, eyeing the Massachusetts orator with a sphinx-like expression which disclosed no hint of either approval or disapproval.

For three hours and eleven minutes, with only a few references to his extensive notes, Daniel Webster pleaded the Union's cause. Relating the grievances of each side, he asked for conciliation and understanding in the name of patriotism. The Senate's main concern, he insisted, was neither to promote slavery nor to abolish it, but to preserve the United States of America. And with telling logic and remarkable foresight he bitterly attacked the idea of "peaceable secession":

Sir, your eyes and mine are never destined to see that miracle. The dismemberment of this vast country without convulsion! Who is so foolish . . . as to expect to see any such thing? . . . Instead of speaking of the possibility or utility of secession, instead of dwelling in those caverns of darkness, . . . let us enjoy the fresh air of liberty and union. . . . Let us make our generation one of the strongest and brightest links in that golden chain which is destined, I fondly believe, to grapple the people of all the states to this Constitution for ages to come.

There was no applause. Buzzing and astonished whispering, yes, but no applause. Perhaps his hearers were too intent—or too astonished. A reporter rushed to the telegraph office. "Mr. Webster has assumed a great responsibility," he wired his paper, "and whether he succeeds or fails, the courage with which he has come forth at least entitles him to the respect of the country."

Daniel Webster did succeed. Even though his speech was repudiated by many in the North, the very fact that one who represented such a belligerent constituency would appeal for understanding in the name of unity and patriotism was recognized in Washington and throughout the South as a *bona fide* assurance of Southern rights. Despite Calhoun's own intransigence, his Charleston *Mercury* praised Webster's address as "noble in language, generous and conciliatory in tone. Mr. Calhoun's clear and powerful exposition would have had something of a decisive effect if it had not been so soon followed by Mr. Webster's masterly playing." And the New Orleans *Picayune* hailed Webster for "the moral courage to do what he believes to be just in itself and necessary for the peace and safety of the country."

And so the danger of immediate secession and bloodshed passed. As Senator Winthrop remarked, Webster's speech had "disarmed and quieted the South [and] knocked the Nashville Convention into a cocked hat." The *Journal of Commerce* was to remark in later months that "Webster did more than any other man in the whole country, and at a greater hazard of personal popularity, to stem and roll back the torrent of sectionalism which in 1850 threatened to overthrow the pillars of the Constitution and the Union."

Some historians—particularly those who wrote in the latter half of the nineteenth century under the influence of the moral earnestness of Webster's articulate Abolitionist foes—do not agree with Allan Nevins, Henry Steele Commager, Gerald Johnson and others who have praised the Seventh of March speech as "the highest statesmanship . . . Webster's last great service to the nation." Many deny that secession would have occurred in 1850 without such compromises; and others maintain that subsequent events proved eventual secession was inevitable regardless of what compromises were made. But still others insist that delaying war for ten years narrowed the issues between North and South and in the long run helped preserve the Union. The spirit of conciliation in Webster's speech gave the North the righteous feeling that it had made every attempt to treat the South with fairness, and the defenders of the Union were thus united more strongly against what they felt to be Southern violations of those compromises ten years later. Even from the military point of view of the North, postponement of the battle for ten years enabled the Northern states to increase tremendously their lead in population, voting power, production and railroads.

Undoubtedly this was understood by many of Webster's supporters, including the business and professional men of Massachusetts who helped distribute hundreds of thousands of copies of the Seventh of March speech throughout the country. It was understood by Daniel Webster, who dedicated the printed copies to the people of Massachusetts with these words: "Necessity compels me to speak true rather than pleasing things. . . . I should indeed like to please you; but I prefer to save you, whatever be your attitude toward me."

But it was not understood by the Abolitionists and Free Soilers of 1850. Few politicians have had the distinction of being scourged by such talented constituents. The Rev. Theodore Parker, heedless of the dangers of secession, who had boasted of harboring a fugitive slave in his cellar and writing his sermons with a sword over his ink stand and a pistol in his desk "loaded and ready for defense," denounced Webster in merciless fashion from his pulpit, an attack he would continue even after Webster's death: "No living man has done so much," he cried, "to debauch the conscience of the nation. . . . I know of no deed in American history done by a son of New England to which I can compare this, but the act of Benedict Arnold." "Webster," said Horace Mann, "is a fallen star! Lucifer descending from Heaven!" Longfellow asked the world: "Is it possible? Is this the Titan who hurled mountains at Hayne years ago?" And Emerson proclaimed that "Every drop of blood in that man's veins has eyes that look downward. . . . Webster's absence of moral faculty is degrading to the country." To William Cullen Bryant, Webster was "a man who has deserted the cause which he lately defended, and deserted it under circumstances which force upon him the imputation of a sordid motive." And to James Russell Lowell he was "the most meanly and foolishly treacherous man I ever heard of."

Charles Sumner, who would be elevated to the Senate upon his departure, enrolled the name of Webster on "the dark list of apostates. Mr. Webster's elaborate treason has done more than anything else to break down the North." Senator William H. Seward, the brilliant "Conscience" Whig, called Webster a "traitor to the cause of freedom." A mass meeting in Faneuil Hall condemned the speech as "unworthy of a wise statesman and a good man," and resolved that "Constitution or no Constitution, law or no law, we will not allow a fugitive slave to be taken from the state of Massachusetts." As the Massachusetts Legislature enacted further resolutions wholly contrary to the spirit of the Seventh of March speech, one member called Webster "a recreant son of Massachusetts who misrepresents her in the Senate"; and another stated that "Daniel Webster will be a fortunate man if God, in his sparing mercy, shall preserve his life long enough for him to repent of this act and efface this stain on his name."

The Boston *Courier* pronounced that it was "unable to find that any Northern Whig member of Congress concurs with Mr. Webster"; and his old defender, the Boston *Atlas,* stated, "His sentiments are not our sentiments nor we venture to say of the Whigs of New England." The New York *Tribune* considered it "unequal to the occasion and unworthy of its author"; the New York *Evening Post* spoke in terms of a "traitorous retreat . . . a man who deserted the cause which he lately defended"; and the Abolitionist press called it "the scarlet infamy of Daniel Webster. . . . An indescribably base and wicked speech."

Edmund Quincy spoke bitterly of the "ineffable meanness of the lion turned spaniel in his fawnings on the masters whose hands he was licking for the sake of the dirty puddings they might have to toss to him." And finally, the name of Daniel Webster was humiliated for all time in the literature of our land by the cutting words of the usually gentle John Greenleaf Whittier in his immortal poem "Ichabod":

> So fallen! so lost! the light withdrawn
> Which once he wore!
> The glory from his gray hairs gone
> Forevermore! . . .
>
> Of all we loved and honored, naught
> Save power remains;
> A fallen angel's pride of thought,
> Still strong in chains. . . .
>
> Then pay the reverence of old days
> To his dead fame;
> Walk backward, with averted gaze,
> And hide the shame!

Years afterward Whittier was to recall that he penned this acid verse "in one of the saddest moments of my life." And for Daniel Webster, the arrogant, scornful giant of the ages who believed himself above political rancor, Whittier's attack was especially bitter. To some extent he had attempted to shrug off his attackers, stating that he had expected to be libeled and abused, particularly by the Abolitionists and intellectuals who had previously scorned him, much as George Washington and others before him had been abused. To those who urged a prompt reply, he merely related the story of the old deacon in a similar predicament who told his friends, "I always make it a rule never to clean up the path until the snow is done falling."

But he was saddened by the failure of a single other New England Whig to rise to his defense, and he remarked that he was

> engaged in a controversy in which I have neither a leader nor a follower from among my own immediate friends. . . . I am tired of standing up here, almost alone from Massachusetts, contending for practical measures absolutely essential to the good of the country. . . . For five months . . . no one of my colleagues manifested the slightest concurrence in my statements. . . . Since the 7th of March there has not been an hour in which I have not felt a crushing weight of anxiety. I have sat down to no breakfast or dinner to which I have brought an unconcerned and easy mind.

But, although he sought to explain his objectives and reassure his friends of his continued opposition to slavery, he nevertheless insisted he would

> stand on the principle of my speech to the end. . . . If necessary I will take the stump in every village in New England. . . . What is to come of the present commotion in men's minds I cannot foresee; but my own convictions of duty are fixed and strong, and I shall continue to follow those convictions without faltering. . . . In highly excited times it is far easier to fan and feed the flames of discord, than to subdue them; and he who counsels moderation is in danger of being regarded as failing in his duty to his party.

And the following year, despite his seventy years, Webster went on extended speaking tours defending his position: "If the chances had been one in a thousand that Civil War would be the result, I should still have felt that thousandth chance should be guarded against by any reasonable sacrifice." When his efforts—and those of Clay, Douglas and others—on behalf of compromise were ultimately successful, he noted sarcastically that many of his colleagues were now saying "They always meant to stand by the Union to the last."

But Daniel Webster was doomed to disappointment in his hopes that this latent support might again enable him to seek the Presidency. For his speech had so thoroughly destroyed those prospects that the recurring popularity of his position could not possibly satisfy the great masses of voters in New England and the North. He could not receive the Presidential nomination he had so long desired; but neither could he ever put to rest the assertion, which was not only expressed by his contemporary critics but subsequently by several nineteenth-century historians, that his real objective in the Seventh of March speech was a bid for Southern support for the Presidency.

But this "profound selfishness," which Emerson was so certain the speech represented, could not have entered into Daniel Webster's motivations. "Had he been bidding for the Presidency," as Professor Nevins points out, "he would have trimmed his phrases and inserted weasel-words upon New Mexico and the fugitive slaves. The first precaution of any aspirant for the Presidency is to make sure of his own state and section; and Webster knew that his speech would send echoes of denunciation leaping from Mount Mansfield to Monamoy Light." Moreover, Webster was sufficiently acute politically to know that a divided party such as his would turn away from politically controversial figures and move to an uncommitted neutral individual, a principle consistently applied to this day. And the 1852 Whig Convention followed exactly this course. After the procompromise vote had been divided for fifty-two ballots between Webster and President Fillmore, the convention turned to the popular General Winfield Scott. Not a single Southern Whig supported Webster. And when the Boston Whigs urged that the party platform take credit for the Clay Compromise, of which, they said, "Daniel Webster, with the concurrence of Henry Clay and other profound statesmen, was the author," Senator Corwin of Ohio was reported to have commented sarcastically, "And I, with the concurrence of Moses and some extra help, wrote the Ten Commandments."

So Daniel Webster, who neither could have intended his speech as an improvement of his political popularity nor permitted his ambitions to weaken his plea for the Union, died a disappointed and discouraged death in 1852, his eyes fixed on the flag flying from the mast of the sailboat he had anchored in view of his bedroom window. But to the very end he was true to character, asking on his deathbed, "Wife, children, doctor, I trust on this occasion I have said nothing unworthy of Daniel Webster." And to the end he had been true to the Union, and to his greatest act of courageous principle; for in his last words to the Senate, Webster had written his own epitaph:

> I shall stand by the Union . . . with absolute disregard of personal consequences. What are personal consequences . . . in comparison with the good or evil which may befall a great country in a crisis like this? . . . Let the consequences be what they will, I am careless. No man can suffer too much, and no man can fall too soon, if he suffer or if he fall in defense of the liberties and Constitution of his country.

IV

THOMAS HART BENTON

"I Despise the Bubble Popularity . . ."

"Mr. President, sir . . ." A burly, black-haired Senator was speaking to a nearly empty chamber in 1850. Those who remained, including a nervous Senator who had just termed the speaker quarrelsome, saw his great muscles tighten and his sweeping shoulders become icily erect, and heard his hard, cold voice rasp out the word "sir" like a poisoned dart from his massive, Romanesque head.

"Mr. President, sir . . . I never quarrel, sir. But sometimes I fight, sir; and whenever I fight, sir, a funeral follows, sir."

No one regarded this as an idle boast by the senior Senator from Missouri, Thomas Hart Benton. True, he had not killed a man since his early days in St. Louis, when a U.S. District Attorney had the misfortune to engage the rugged Missourian in a duel (at nine feet!). But all the Senate knew that Thomas Hart Benton was a rough and tumble fighter off and on the Senate floor—no longer with pistols but with stinging sarcasm, vituperative though learned oratory and bitterly heated debate.

He himself was immune to the wounds of those political clashes from which his adversaries retired bleeding and broken. For his great ego and vigorous health had made him thick-skinned mentally as well as physically. (The leathery quality of his skin was in part the result of a daily brushing with a horsehair brush "because, sir, the Roman gladiators did it, sir." When asked if the brush was truly rough, he would roar: "Why, sir, if I were to touch you with that brush, sir, you would cry murder, sir!")

But now, with his last term rounding out thirty years in the Senate, Benton was under attack in his final great fight to the finish—and this time the political funeral to follow would be his own. From 1821 to 1844 he had reigned supreme as Kingpin of Missouri politics, her first Senator, her most beloved idol. In the words of one of his opponents, it meant "political death to any man to even whisper a breath against 'old Bullion' " (the nickname derived from Benton's fight for hard money). Although inexpert at politics, constantly the advocate of unpopular issues within his state and gradually out of touch with most of her younger politicians, Benton nevertheless did not even need to ask to be re-elected during that charmed period. The fact that he alone disdained patronage, petty Congressional graft and favors from lobbyists may have disturbed the politicians, but not the people of Missouri! Democratic candidates for the Missouri Legislature were required to pledge to vote for his re-election under pain of humiliating defeat in their own campaigns. The first Senator ever to serve thirty consecutive years, Thomas Hart Benton achieved a prominence which no other Senator from a new state could claim, and he championed the West with a boundless energy no opposing candidate could match. The Pony Express, the telegraph line and the highways to the interior were among his proud accomplishments—and a transcontinental railroad and fully developed

West, rich in population and resources, were among his dreams. Defeat Benton, father of the Senate and defender of the people? "Nobody opposes Benton, sir," he would roar. "Nobody but a few black-jack prairie lawyers; these are the only opponents of Benton. Benton and the people, Benton and Democracy are one and the same, sir; synonymous terms, sir, synonymous terms."

But by 1844, the handwriting of inevitable defeat had already appeared on the wall. Missouri, a slave state, gradually came to feel more strongly that her allegiance belonged to her sister states of the South. She tended to look with increasing suspicion upon her rebellious Senator whose primary loyalty was neither to his party nor his section, but to the Union for which he had fought —on the battlefront and in Congress—and upon the rugged independence of his views for which he intended to fight, in or out of Congress. His devotion to the Union was far greater than his devotion to the South or the Democratic party. (His opponents charged that Benton told the 1844 Democratic National Convention, as it prepared to abandon Van Buren, that he would "see the Democratic party sink 50 fathoms deep into the middle of hell fire before I will give one inch with Mr. Van Buren.")

As the campaign for the legislature which would consider his re-election began in 1844, Benton broke sharply with his state and party by engineering the defeat of the treaty for the annexation of Texas. Convinced that the treaty was a plot hatched by Calhoun without consideration of Mexican rights or resistance, and for political, slavery and secessionist purposes, Benton—who actually favored Western expansion on the nationalistic grounds of "manifest destiny"—was handing his political enemies a choice opportunity to assail him openly. The Texas Treaty was popular in Missouri, despite Benton's assertion that he did not know whether his constituents really were opposed to his position:

if there were, and I knew it, I should resign my place; for I could neither violate their known wishes in voting against it, nor violate my own sense of constitutional or moral duty in voting for it. If the alternative should be the extinction of my political life, I should have to embrace it.

Labeled a traitor to his party and section and an ally of the Whigs and British, Benton openly lost the support of prominent candidates for the Missouri Legislature and was subject to all manner of personal attacks—as a nonresident, a defaulter in his debts, and one contemptuous of public opinion. Senator Benton, declared the Missouri *Register*, is "a demagogue and a tyrant at heart . . . the greatest egotist in Christendom. . . . Wherever he goes, whatever he does, he shows but one characteristic—that of a blustering, insolent, unscrupulous demagogue."

But Benton did not hesitate even on the eve of election to continue his denunciation of his party's Texas policy. He charged on the Senate floor that his political opposition in Missouri had been stirred up by Calhoun, Tyler and their friends, including "300 newspapers in the pay of the Department of State, many of them not visibly so." His tremendous personal popularity among the ordinary citizens carried him through the legislature—but by only eight votes, in a legislature his party controlled by a twenty-seven vote margin. At the same time, the proslavery Democrat Atchison was elected to fill an unexpired Senate term by a margin of thirty-four votes. Senator Benton could hardly mistake the ominous unwritten instructions of his state—in effect: "temper your independent tongue, sir, and stand by the South, or suffer the inevitable consequences."

But a hardy youth on the Tennessee frontier had not taught Thomas Hart Benton how to avoid a fight, whether with wild beasts, neighbors or politicians. (His brutal free-for-all with Andrew Jackson, which caused him to leave a promising legal and political career in

Tennessee for Missouri, was a subject of much comment when the two became firm political and personal friends in Washington. And years later, when Benton was asked by a novice whether he had known Jackson, he haughtily replied: "Yes, sir, I knew him, sir; General Jackson was a very great man, sir. I shot him, sir. Afterward he was of great use to me, sir, in my battle with the United States Bank.") Like a "wild buffalo"—some said a "gnarled oak"—he returned to the Senate convinced that the entire nation depended upon him to carry the attack on every issue every day.

Despite his near defeat in 1844-45, Senator Benton audaciously opposed his party and state on the Oregon expansion issue. Having personally aroused intense public approval for expansion—particularly in Missouri, which had sent large numbers of its citizens to Oregon—he now felt that the Democratic "whole of Oregon or none," "fifty-four forty or fight" position was extravagantly unrealistic. Counseling President Polk against adhering to those slogans in dealing with England and Canada, he assailed his Democratic colleagues in the Senate for their refusal to concede the error of their views—especially Michigan's Lewis Cass. Explaining that the "simples" was a kind of disease which made Missouri horses physically and mentally blind, and which could be cured only when the veterinary cut a certain nerve, he announced that he had "cut Cass for the simples, sir, and cured him."

Again he was assailed as a coward and traitor. His biographer believes that "probably no man in history has been more vilified than he was at this time."

But Benton pursued his independent and increasingly lonely course. He would not go over to the Whig party, whose petty politicians, he said, "are no more able to comprehend me . . . than a rabbit, which breeds 12 times a year, could comprehend the gestation of an elephant which carries 2 years." Nor would he seek financial aid from the lobbyists swarming over Washington, telling the agent for one group seeking a ship subsidy that the only condition upon which he would lift a finger to help was "when the vessels are finished they will be used to take all such damned rascals as you, sir, out of the country." Nor would he make peace with the Missouri political chiefs, carrying his dislike for the St. Louis postmaster to the point where he resorted to the express company for any mail he thought Postmaster Armstrong might possibly handle.

Only at home was Benton at peace with the world. As his daughter, Jessie Benton Frémont, wrote in her memoirs: "To him home brought the strength of peace and repose, and he never suffered the outside public atmosphere of strife to enter there." But his family life was clouded by the death of his two sons early in life, and by the long physical and mental illness of the wife to whom he was at all times tender and devoted. On one occasion, which revealed the depth of warm devotion which lay beneath that rough conceit, Benton was entertaining a French prince and other distinguished guests when his wife, not fully dressed, rambled into the room and stared adoringly at her husband. Interrupting the embarrassed silence that followed, Senator Benton with dignity and majesty introduced his wife to the prince and others, seated her by his side, and resumed conversation.

But in the Senate he was alone, hard and merciless. With piles of books and papers heaped on his desk, speaking frequently to nearly empty galleries and an indifferent chamber, Benton poured forth thousands of statistics, classical illustrations and magnificent metaphors upon colleagues with far more formal schooling and originality of thought. As an obituary notice later described it:

> With a readiness which was often surprising he could quote from a Roman law or a Greek philosopher, from Virgil's Georgics, the Arabian Nights, Herodotus or Sancho

Panza, from the Sacred Carpets, the German Reformers or Adam Smith; from Fénelon or Hudibras, from the Financial Reports of Necca, or the doings of the Council of Trent; from the debates of the adoption of the Constitution, or the intrigues of the kitchen cabinet, or from some forgotten speech of a deceased member of Congress.

Benton, with but one year at the University of North Carolina, was said to carry the Congressional Library in his head; and he achieved great satisfaction, if another Senator forgot a name or date, by obtaining from the library some obscure volume, marking the exact page on which the correct information appeared and sending it to his colleague. His own thirst for knowledge, particularly about the unsettled West, was unquenchable, and led him not only to books but also, a contemporary tells us, to "hunters and trappers, scouts, wild half-breeds, Indian chiefs, and Jesuit missionaries."

But no amount of acquired information, bulldog persistence or ferocious egotism could save Thomas Hart Benton from the tidal wave that engulfed the Senate and his state over one burning issue—slavery. Unfortunately, until it was too late, Benton refused to recognize slavery as a major issue, believed that the Missouri Compromise of 1820 (which brought his state into the Union and Benton to the Senate) had taken it out of politics, and refused to debate it on the Senate floor. "I cannot degrade the Senate by engaging in slavery and disunion discussions," he said. "Silence such debate is my prayer; and if that cannot be done, I silence myself." One of the few members of Congress who still brought his slaves with him to his Washington household, he nevertheless was equally opposed to the Abolitionists and the secessionists, to the permanent extension of this evil into new territory by the South and to the partisan exploitation of its miseries by Northern agitators. Above all, he was most distressed about the fact that the issue was constantly raised by both sides as a barrier to Western expansion and the admission of new states to the Union.

The beginning of Benton's end—so strongly suggested already by the antagonisms he had aroused over Texas and Oregon—came on February 19, 1847. John C. Calhoun read to a worried Senate his famous resolutions insisting that Congress had no right to interfere with the development of slavery in the territories. Later events indicated the correctness of Benton's views that those resolutions were but "firebrands intended for electioneering and disunion purposes," providing the slave states with a program on which to unite—not only as a section but behind the leadership and Presidential candidacy of Calhoun himself. Nevertheless, Calhoun called for an immediate vote; and in the momentary confusion that followed, he was angrily amazed to see the massive and stately Benton rising from his chair, his face flashing with obvious contempt for Calhoun, the resolutions and his own political fate.

MR. BENTON: Mr. President, we have some business to transact, and I do not intend to avoid business for a string of abstractions.

MR. CALHOUN: . . . I certainly supposed the Senator from Missouri, the representative of a slaveholding state, would have supported these resolutions . . .

MR. BENTON: The Senator knows very well from my whole course in public life that I would never leave public business to take up firebrands to set the world on fire.

MR. CALHOUN: Then I shall know where to find the gentleman.

MR. BENTON: I shall be found in the right place . . . on the side of my country and the Union. ["This answer," wrote Benton in later years, "given on that day and on that spot, is one of the incidents of his life which Mr. Benton will wish posterity to remember."]

When Calhoun initiated a series of secret, nightly meetings of Congressmen from slave states, strongly supported by Benton's Missouri colleague Atchison, Benton refused to have anything to do with it. When Calhoun's colleague from South Carolina challenged him to a duel, he refused to have anything to do with him. When he was warned not to deliver his great eulogy in appreciation of that foe of slavery, John Quincy Adams, he refused to heed such warnings. And finally, when in 1848 the slavery issue split the Democratic party at its convention, Benton, deploring the split and denying the importance of the issue, refused to support either camp actively. He was now a man without a party, a politician without a recognized platform, and a Senator without a constituency.

The noose was set early in 1849. Calhoun, successful in obtaining adoption of his resolutions by several Southern legislatures, denounced Benton to his Missouri enemies as one "false to the South for the last ten years. . . . He can do us much less injury in the camp of the abolitionists than he could in our own camp. His will be the fate of all traitors." By an overwhelming margin, the Missouri Legislature adopted Calhoun's resolutions, expressed Missouri's desire to cooperate with other slaveholding states, and instructed her Senators to vote accordingly. Outraged at this setback, Benton charged that the resolutions had been inspired in Washington and falsified real opinion in Missouri. They were, he said, "the speckled progeny of a vile conjunction, redolent with lurking treason to the Union":

> Between them and me, henceforth and forever, a high wall and a deep ditch! And no communion, no compromise, no caucus with them. . . . From this command I appeal to the people of Missouri, and if they confirm the instructions, I shall give them an opportunity to find a Senator to carry their wishes into effect, as I cannot do anything to dissolve this Union, or to array one-half of it against the other.

Determined to see the Legislature's resolutions withdrawn or repudiated, Benton launched an aggressive tour of his hostile state. He denounced the leading Southern spokesman for his party as "John 'Cataline' Calhoun" (a denunciation he would continue until shortly before Calhoun's death after a long illness in 1850. He withheld his attack then, he said, because "When God Almighty lays his hand upon a man, sir, I take mine off, sir"). Pouring out his taunting sarcasm in short, bombastic thunderbolts of gigantic rage, hate and ridicule, day after day, in town after town, he assailed his opponents and their policies with bitter invective. His overbearing and merciless roughness, personal vindictiveness and uncompromising enmity drove away many whose support he might otherwise have won by conciliation. Beginning his address to crowded meetings with "My friends—and in that term I comprehend those who come to hear the truth and to believe it—none others," he attacked the resolutions as "false in their facts, incendiary in their temper, disunion in their object, high treason in their remedy, and usurpation in their character. . . . The whole concept, concoction and passage of the resolutions were perfected by fraud . . . a plot to get me out of the Senate and out of the way of the disunion plotters." Attacking his long-time political enemy, Judge Napton, who had reportedly drawn up the resolutions, he said that any man who acted according to the provisions of those measures would "be subject to be hung under the laws of the United States—and if a judge will *deserve* to be hung."

One day, bitterly reading and commenting upon the names of each member of the Legislature, he stopped when he came to the "D's" and said he smelled a Nullifier. A legislator named Davies having arisen to protest, Benton scowled: "I never called your name, sir. Turn your profile to the audience. . . . [Like a fool, Davies complied] . . . Citizens, that is not the profile of a man; it is the profile of a dog." When an old friend, accidentally failing to remove his hat, asked a question in the middle of a speech, Benton angrily scolded, "Who is this man, citizens, who dares to stop Benton in his speech?" "Aycock, Colonel Aycock," came a dozen voices. "Aycock? No, citizens, no; not a cock; but a hen rather. Take off your hat, sir, and take your seat."

In another town, spotting from the platform three of his enemies sitting quietly in his audience while he characterized their resolutions as "fungus cancers," he caustically referred to them by name "as demure as three prostitutes at a christening." When his attention was called to the criticism of a distinguished opponent, he lashed back, "Send him word that Benton says he lied from the bottom of his belly to the root of his tongue." And when, upon his ignoring the greeting of a former friend who had disapproved of his course, that unfortunate gentleman bowed and reminded him of his name, Benton coldly replied: "Sir, Benton once knew a man by that name, but he is dead, yes, sir, he is dead." When he mounted the platform at Fayette, where his life had been threatened if he dared enter the city limits, a body of armed men began an uproar. But according to the Jefferson *Inquirer*, "in a quarter of an hour the insulters were cowed; and the speech for four hours was received with respect and applause."

But Benton's turbulent tour could not stem a tide much greater than any one man or single state. With undisguised glee Calhoun wrote a friend by summer's end:

> It is said that Benton will not be able to sustain himself in Missouri. His colleague General Atchison . . . says that he has as good a chance to be elected Pope as to be elected Senator.

A friend of Benton's, on the other hand, wrote:

> I am sorry Mr. Benton indulges in so much profanity. Yet in this respect his opponents . . . are not a whit behind. Nine out of twenty-two Democratic papers in the state are

unbounded in vilifying him with such epithets as traitor, apostate, scoundrel, barn burner, abolitionist and free-soiler . . . I am afraid Benton will be defeated.

At the close of his tour, confident at least in his outward appearances, Benton addressed a letter to the people of Missouri:

> I know of no cause for this conspiracy against me, except that I am the natural enemy of all rotten politicians. . . . I am for the Union as it is; and for that cause Mr. Calhoun denounced me for a traitor to the South. . . . the signal to all his followers in Missouri to go to work upón me. . . . The conspiracy is now established. . . . Nullification resolutions passed by fraud, which it was known I would not obey. . . . Men appointed to attack me in all parts of the state. . . . Packed meetings got up to condemn me. . . . Newspapers enlisted in the service . . . and many good citizens deceived.

But he could not shame his enemies into submission. In December of 1849, the anti-Benton leaders issued a statement labeling the veteran Senator "reckless, dishonest and unscrupulous . . . a wicked, deliberate and willful liar . . . attempting to betray his party for selfish purposes." And when Congress reassembled, Calhoun was successful in forcing the Democratic caucus to strip Benton of all his committees except Foreign Affairs, on which he was left only for purposes of a trumped-up story that Atchison had graciously interceded for him.

Even his gigantic ego could not have hidden from Thomas Hart Benton the unmistakable fact that this was his last term—unless. Would he initiate a convention of all Missouri Democrats to settle his differences with the proslavery camp? "I would sooner," he thundered, "sit in council with the six thousand dead who have died of cholera in St. Louis than go into convention with such a gang of scamps!" Would he speak one word for the South in the great debate of 1850 on the Clay Compromise, or at least remain silent in order to save the seat he loved for future battles? He would not. As a Missouri associate recalled: ". . . At an early period of his existence, while reading Plutarch, he determined that if it should ever become necessary for the good of his country, he would sacrifice his own political existence."

As the contest for the State Legislature that would name his successor raged in Missouri, Senator Benton stood fast by his post in Washington, outspoken to the end in his condemnation of the views his constituents now embraced. Willing to meet crushing defeat rather than compromise his principles (for as Clay said, intending it to be disparaging, Benton had the "hide of a hippopotamus"), he towered over his more famous colleagues in terms of sheer moral courage. Now isolated from his political friends in the West and South, and yet maintaining his distaste for the Abolitionists, whom he held equally responsible for splitting the Union, Benton steered an extraordinarily independent course in his vituperative attacks on Clay's compromise. Bitterly assailing the collection of measures which formed the "Great Compromise" and scornfully ridiculing its sponsors, he complained when he was constantly called to order by the presiding officer. The so-called compromise, in Benton's opinion, was a hollow sham containing too generous concessions to the Secessionists and unnecessarily involving a subject dear to his heart, California. To extend the slavery line of the Missouri Compromise into California and thus split the state, or to delay its admission by tying it to this Omnibus Bill, was reprehensible to Benton, the father-in-law of Colonel John Frémont, hero of California's exploration and development. What if California's admission were prevented by the failure of the compromise, he asked?

MR. BENTON: . . . Who then is to be blamed? I do not ask these questions of the Senator from Kentucky [Mr. Clay]. It might be unlawful to do so; for, by the law of the land, no man is bound to criminate himself.

MR. CLAY [from his seat]: I do not claim the benefit of the law.

MR. BENTON: As a law-abiding and generous man, I give him the benefit of the law whether he claims it or not. It is time for him to begin to consider the responsibility he has incurred in jumbling California up in this crowd, where she is sure to meet death. . . . Mr. President, it is time to be done with this comedy of errors. California is suffering for want of admission. New Mexico is suffering for want of protection. The public business is suffering for want of attention. The character of Congress is suffering for want of progress in business. It is time to put an end to so many evils, and I have made the motion to move the indefinite postponement of this unmanageable mass of incongruous bills, each an impediment to the other, that they may be taken up one by one to receive the decision which their respective merits require.

During the course of the year, still another melodramatic event—termed "the greatest indignity the Senate had ever suffered"—served to show the bitter feelings of the South toward Benton. The peppery Senator Henry Foote of Mississippi, no blind follower of Calhoun but suspected by Benton of helping plot his defeat in Missouri, took the floor on several occasions to abuse Benton's position in a coarse manner exceeding even the Missourian's own rhetorical excesses. Taunting him with his approaching defeat in Missouri, and stinging under Benton's counterattack, Foote ridiculed Benton as one "shielded by his age . . . and shielded by his own established cowardice."

Finally Benton announced that, if the Senate failed to protect him from such "false and cowardly" attacks, he intended "to protect himself, cost what it may." On April 17, in the midst of another verbal assault upon him by Foote, Benton advanced toward the Mississippian, then turned back at a colleague's restraining touch. Suddenly

Foote whipped out a pistol and pointed it at Benton, who dramatically threw open his coat and cried: "I have no pistol! Let him fire! Let the assassin fire!"

No one fired. The Senate was shocked—although its special committee on censure barely rapped the knuckles of the two participants—but verbal assaults between the two did not cease. When Benton heard of Foote's threat that he intended to write a small book in which *l'affaire* Benton would play a leading role, Benton replied: "Tell Foote that I shall write a very large book in which he will not figure at all!" (And he did.) And Foote, referring tauntingly to Benton's expected defeat in Missouri, cried to the Senate: "If we have been the subjects of tyranny, and if we have borne it with patience for years, yes, sir, for almost 30 years, thank God! we may exclaim at last, 'Behold the tyrant prostrate in the dust, and Rome again is free.' "

Foote's expectations were fully realized. Benton's vote against dividing California was his last act of importance in the Senate. In January, 1851, climaxing a bitter twelve-day struggle among its three distinct parties—Benton Democrats, anti-Benton Democrats and Whigs—the Missouri Legislature on its fortieth ballot elected a Whig. After thirty years of outstanding statesmanship in the Senate of the United States, Thomas Hart Benton was ignominiously dismissed from the service and called home.

Undismayed, and still stubbornly refusing to follow the easy path to a graceful and popular political retirement, Benton fought to return to Congress the following year as Representative from St. Louis. His campaign, according to the opposition New Orleans *Crescent,* "spared no public or personal denunciation. He exhausted every expletive of abuse. He ransacked the entire range of the English language for terms of scorn and derision." Elected in one final burst of personal popularity, he promptly threw to the winds all chances for future re-election by delivering one of his most memorable, and one of his most vituperative, speeches in opposition to the chief measure of his party, the Kansas-Nebraska Bill. With violent invective he denounced provisions repealing his cherished Missouri Compromise and pleaded for a national outlook. "He votes as a Southern man," he commented on the remarks of a member from Georgia, "and votes sectionally. I also am a Southern man, but vote nationally on national issues. . . . I am Southern by my birth—Southern in my convictions, interests and connections, and I shall abide the fate of the South in everything in which she has *right* on her side."

Soundly defeated for re-election in 1854, and grieved by the death of his beloved wife, Benton was not yet ready to submit. In vain he sought re-election to the Senate in 1855; and, at the age of 74, made one last, hopeless race for Governor in 1856. Jessie Benton Frémont revealed in her memoirs that her courageous father, suffering from what he knew to be a fatal throat cancer, could speak in public only by maintaining absolute silence for several days in advance. Even then his throat bled during and following his still ferocious speeches. Yet he traveled more than twelve hundred miles in a desperate speaking tour to defeat the Whig and anti-Benton Democratic candidates, and he returned home, defeated but proud, to complete his monumental historical works.

That flamboyant ego, for which he was both loved and despised, never deserted him. When the publishers of his *Thirty Years' View* sent a messenger to inquire as to how many copies he thought ought to be printed, he loftily replied: "Sir, they can ascertain from the last census how many families there are in the United States, sir"; and that was the only suggestion he would make. In introducing his work, Benton states that "the bare enumeration of the measures of which he was the author and the prime promoter, would be almost a history of Congress Legislation. . . . The long list is known throughout the length and breadth of the land—repeated with the familiarity of household words . . . and studied by the little boys who feel an honorable ambition beginning to stir within their bosoms . . ."

He died while still hard at work, using an amanuensis when his feeble hands could no longer grasp a pen, and uncomplaining even to his last whispered words: "I am comfortable, I am content." His death, mourned throughout the nation, revealed how little wealth his upright career had accumulated for his daughters.

But even in death and defeat, Thomas Hart Benton was victorious. For his voice from the past on behalf of Union was one of the deciding factors that prevented Missouri from yielding to all the desperate efforts to drive her into secession along with her sister slave states. Fate had borne out the wisdom of Benton's last report to his constituents as Senator: "I value solid popularity—the esteem of good men for good action. I despise the bubble popularity that is won without merit and lost without crime. . . . I have been Senator 30 years. . . . I sometimes had to act against the preconceived opinions and first impressions of my constituents; but always with full reliance upon their intelligence to understand me and their equity to do me justice—*and I have never been disappointed.*"

V

SAM HOUSTON

". . . I Can Forget That I Am Called a Traitor."

The first rays of dawn were streaking into the ill-lit Senate chamber of 1854 as one final speaker rose to seek recognition. Weary, haggard and unshaven Senators, slumped despondently in their chairs after the rigors of an all-night session, muttered "Vote, Vote" in the hopes of discouraging any further oratory on a bill already certain of passage. But Senator Sam Houston of Texas, the hero of San Jacinto, was not easily discouraged by overwhelming odds; and as his deep, musical voice carried the bold if unpolished words of a powerful message to his astonished colleagues, they shook off the dull stupor which had deadened their fatigued brains and sat upright and attentive.

The bill on which bitter and exhausting debate now closed was known as the Kansas-Nebraska Bill, the new "unity" device of the Democratic party and the latest concession to the South. It repealed the Missouri Compromise of 1820, and reopened the slavery extension issue thought settled in the Compromise of 1850, by permitting the residents of that vast territory from Iowa to the Rockies to decide the slavery question for themselves, on the assumption that the northern part of the territory would be free and the southern part slave. For Democrats and Southerners, this bill had become "must" legislation.

Sam Houston was a Democrat of long standing. And Sam Houston was a Southerner by birth, residence, loyalty and philosophy. But Sam Houston was also Sam Houston, one of the most independent, unique, popular, forceful and dramatic individuals ever to enter the Senate chamber. The first Senator from Texas, his name had long before been a household word as Commander in Chief of those straggling and undermanned Texas volunteers who routed the entire Mexican Army at San Jacinto, captured its general and established the independence of Texas. He had been acclaimed as the first President of the Independent Republic of Texas, a Member of her Congress, and President again before the admission of Texas into the Union as a state. He was no easy mark at the age of sixty-four, and neither sectional nor party ties were enough to seal his lips.

Sam Houston looked upon the Missouri Compromise, which he had supported in 1820 as a youthful Congressman from Tennessee, as a solemn and sacred compact between North and South, in effect a part of the Constitution when Texas was admitted into the Union. Nor was he willing to discard the Compromise of 1850, which he had supported despite the enmity of Texas fire-eaters who called his vote "the damnedest outrage yet committed upon Texas." With rugged, homely but earnest eloquence, he begged his weary colleagues in an impromptu plea not to plunge the nation into new agitations over the slavery issue.

Sam Houston must have known the bill would pass, he must have known that not a single other Southern Democrat would join him, he must have known that, as rumor of his position had spread the previous week, the

Richmond *Enquirer* had spoken for his constituents in declaring, "Nothing can justify this treachery; nor can anything save the traitor from the deep damnation which such treason may merit." But, standing erect, his chin thrust forward, picturesque if not eccentric in his military cloak and pantherskin waistcoat (at times he appeared in a vast sombrero and Mexican blanket), Sam Houston, the "magnificent barbarian," made one of his rare speeches to a weary but attentive Senate:

> This is an eminently perilous measure; and do you expect me to remain here silent, or to shrink from the discharge of my duty in admonishing the South of what I conceive the results will be? I will speak in spite of all the intimidations, or threats, or discountenances that may be thrown upon me. Sir, the charge that I am going with the Abolitionists or Free-Soilers affects me not. The discharge of conscious duty prompts me often to confront the united array of the very section of the country in which I reside, in which my associations are, in which my affections rest. . . . Sir, if this is a boon that is offered to propitiate the South, I, as a Southern man, repudiate it. I will have none of it. . . . Our children are either to live in after times in the enjoyment of peace, of harmony, and prosperity, or the alternative remains for them of anarchy, discord, and civil broil. We can avert the last. I trust we shall. . . . I adjure you to regard the contract once made to harmonize and preserve this Union. Maintain the Missouri Compromise! Stir not up agitation! Give us peace!

"It was," Houston was later to remark, "the most unpopular vote I ever gave [but] the wisest and most patriotic." Certainly it was the most unpopular. When old Sam had first journeyed to the Senate, the baby-new state of Texas was primarily concerned with railroad, land, debt and boundary questions, without particularly strong Southern ties. But now, Texas with 150,000 valuable slaves and an overwhelmingly Democratic population consisting largely of citizens from other Southern states, identified its interests with those Houston had attacked; and with near unanimity, she cried for

Houston's scalp as one who had "betrayed his state in the Senate," "joined the Abolitionists" and "deserted the South." By a vote of 73 to 3 the Legislature applauded Houston's colleague for supporting the Nebraska Bill, and condemned the stand of him who was once the most glorious hero the state had ever known. The Democratic State Convention denounced the great warrior as "not in accordance with the sentiments of the Democracy of Texas." The Dallas *Herald* demanded that Houston resign the seat to which Texans had proudly sent him, instead of "retaining a position he has forefeited by misrepresenting them. . . . Let him heed for once the voice of an outraged, misrepresented, and betrayed constituency, so that Texas may for once have a united voice and present an undivided front in the Senate."

To make matters worse, this was not the first offense for Senator Sam Houston, merely—as described by the indignant Clarksville *Standard*—"the last feather that broke the camel's back." He had tangled with John Calhoun on the Oregon question, describing himself as a Southerner for whom "the Union was his guiding star," and who had "no fear that the North would seek to destroy the South notwithstanding the papers signed by old men and women and pretty girls." "The South has been beaten by the South—if united, she would have conquered!" cried an influential Dixie paper when Calhoun rebuked Houston and Benton for providing the winning margin for his opponents. But Sam Houston would only reply: "I know neither North nor South; I know only the Union."

He would have nothing to do, moreover, with Calhoun's "hands-off" slavery resolutions and "Southern Address," attacking that revered sage of the South for his "long-cherished and ill-concealed designs against the Union," and insisting to the Senate that he, Sam Houston, was "on this floor representative of the whole American people." But the Texas Legislature adopted Calhoun's resolutions, and cast a suspicious eye on the ambitious former President of Texas whose name was being mentioned, in the North as well as the South, for the White House in 1852 or 1856.

Finally, Houston had been the first prominent Senator to attack Calhoun's opposition to the Clay Compromise of 1850, quoting the Scripture to label those threatening secession as mere "raging waves of sea, foaming out their own shame. . . ."

> Think you, sir, after the difficulties Texans have encountered to get into the Union, that you can whip them out of it? No, sir . . . we shed our blood to get into it. . . . We were among the last to come into the Union, and being in, we will be the last to get out. . . . I call on the friends of the Union from every quarter to come forward like men, and to sacrifice their differences upon the common altar of their country's good, and to form a bulwark around the Constitution that cannot be shaken. It will require manly efforts, sir, and they must expect to meet with prejudices that will assail them from every quarter. They must stand firm to the Union, regardless of all personal consequences.

Thus his lonely vote against the Kansas-Nebraska Bill, on that stormy dawn in 1854, was indeed the "last straw." It was loudly whispered about the Senate that this was the last term for the colorful General. Those illustrious Senators with whom he had served, whose oratory could not attract the glory and romance which surrounded the name of Sam Houston, may have frowned upon his eccentric dress and his habit of whittling pine sticks on the Senate floor while muttering at the length of senatorial speeches. But they could not help but admire his stoical courage and rugged individualism, which his preface to a brief autobiographical sketch expressed more simply: "This book will lose me some friends. But if it lost me all and gained me none, in

God's name, as I am a free man, I would publish it. . . ."

* * *

The contradictions in the life of Sam Houston a century ago may seem irreconcilable today. Although there are available endless collections of diaries, speeches and letters which throw light on every facet of his life and accomplishments, yet in the center of the stage Houston himself remains shadowed and obscured, an enigma to his friends in his own time, a mystery to the careful historian of today. We may read a letter or a diary in which for a moment he seemed to have dropped his guard, but when we have finished we know little more than before. No one can say with precision by what star Sam Houston steered—his own, Texas' or the nation's.

He was fiercely ambitious, yet at the end he sacrificed for principle all he had ever won or wanted. He was a Southerner, and yet he steadfastly maintained his loyalty to the Union. He was a slaveholder who defended the right of Northern ministers to petition Congress against slavery; he was a notorious drinker who took the vow of temperance; he was an adopted son of the Cherokee Indians who won his first military honors fighting the Creeks; he was a Governor of Tennessee but a Senator from Texas. He was in turn magnanimous yet vindictive, affectionate yet cruel, eccentric yet self-conscious, faithful yet opportunistic. But Sam Houston's contradictions actually confirm his one basic, consistent quality; indomitable individualism, sometimes spectacular, sometimes crude, sometimes mysterious, but always courageous. He could be all things to all men—and yet, when faced with his greatest challenge, he was faithful to himself and to Texas. The turmoil within Sam Houston was nothing more than the turmoil which racked the United States in those stormy years before the Civil War, the colorful uniqueness of Sam Houston was nothing more than the primitive expression of the frontier he had always known.

When still a dreamy and unmanageable boy, he had run away from his Tennessee frontier home, and was adopted by the Cherokee Indians, who christened him Co-lon-neh, the Raven. An infantry officer under Andrew Jackson in 1813, his right arm had been shredded by enemy bullets when he alone had dashed into enemy lines at the battle of the Horseshoe, his men cowering in the hills behind him. A natural actor with a strikingly handsome figure and a flair for picturesque dress and speech, he was a rapidly rising success in Tennessee as prosecuting attorney, Congressman and finally Governor at thirty-five. The story of his sudden resignation as Governor at the height of a popularity which his friend Jackson hoped would make Houston President is shrouded in mystery. Apparently he discovered but a few days after his marriage that his young and beautiful bride had been forced to accept his hand by an ambitious father, when in truth she loved another. His mind and spirit shattered, Houston had abandoned civilization for the Cherokees, drunken debauchery and political and personal exile. Several years later, his balance and purpose restored, General Jackson to whom he was always faithful sent him to Texas, where his fantastic military exploits became as much a part of American folklore as Valley Forge and Gettysburg. But neither adventure, adulation nor a happy second marriage ever banished the inner sadness and melancholy which seemed to some in 1856, now that political defeat approached, more evident than ever.

* * *

But Sam Houston was not one to sit morosely brooding until the whispers of impending defeat were replaced by the avalanche that would crush him. He had already made several tours of Texas during the Senate's autumn recesses, comparing Calhoun with "reckless demagogues," terming Jefferson Davis "ambitious as Lucifer and cold as a lizard," and denouncing with equal vigor both "the mad fanaticism of the North" and "the mad ambition of the South." Many years of living among half-civilized Indian tribes had not made him a respecter of high office; in earlier years he had physically assaulted a Congressional foe of his idol, Andrew Jackson. (He later told friends it made him feel "meaner than I ever felt in my life. I thought I had gotten hold of a great dog but found a contemptible whining puppy.")

Now he struck out with one grand assault on Texas officialdom by announcing himself a candidate for Governor in the 1857 election. He would not run as a Democrat, or as the candidate of any faction or newspaper—or even resign from the Senate. He would run as Sam Houston, to "regenerate the politics of the state. The people want excitement and I had as well give it as anyone."

And plenty of excitement is what he provided, in the first real battle solidly Democratic Texas had ever known. Frequently peeling off his shirt during the hot summer campaign, he harangued audiences in every corner of Texas with his great fund of vituperative epithets and withering sarcasm. Well over six feet tall, still straight as an arrow with massive yet graceful muscles, his penetrating eyes flashed scorn for his opponents and derision of their policies as he reveled in the exercise of the sharp tongue which the dignities of the Senate chamber had largely stilled. One of his speeches was described —by an opposition newspaper, but undoubtedly with some accuracy—as "a compound of abuses and egotism . . . without the sanction of historical truth and . . . without decent and refined language. . . . It was characterized throughout from beginning to end by such epithets as fellow thieves, rascals and assassins." When refused the right to speak in the county courthouse at one stop on his tour, he assured the crowd it was quite all right:

> I am not a taxpayer here. I did not contribute to buy a single brick or nail in this building and have no right to speak here. But if there is a man within the sound of my voice who would desire to hear Sam Houston speak and will follow me to yonder hillside, I have a right to speak on the soil of Texas because I have watered it with my blood.

Denounced on one hand as a traitor and on the other as a Know-Nothing (based on his brief flirtation with that intolerant but nonsectional party), he wrote his wife that "their dirty scandal falls off me like water off a duck's back."

But his votes on Kansas and other Southern measures could not be explained away to an angry constituency, and Texas handed Sam Houston the first trouncing of his political career. He ought to resign from the Senate now, said the antagonistic *Gazette,* instead of "holding on to the barren office . . . merely to receive his per diem allowance." But Sam Houston, encouraged that the margin of his defeat was no greater than three to two, returned to Washington for his final years in the Senate unshaken in his beliefs. When a Southern antagonist taunted him on the Senate floor that his vote against the Kansas-Nebraska Bill had now insured his defeat, Houston merely replied with a graceful smile that it was true "that I have received an earnest and gratifying assurance from my constituents that they intend to relieve me of further service here. . . ." He was not mistaken. On November 10, 1857, Sam Houston was unceremoniously dismissed by the Texas Legislature and a more militant spokesman for the South elected as his successor.

In bidding farewell to his fellow Senators, Houston told his colleagues that he desired to retire "with clean hands and a clean conscience":

> I wish no prouder epitaph to mark the board or slab that may lie on my tomb than this: "He loved his country, he was

a patriot; he was devoted to the Union." If it is for this that I have suffered martyrdom, it is sufficient that I stand at quits with those who have wielded the sacrificial knife.

But we cannot conclude our story of Senator Sam Houston's political courage with his retirement from the Senate. Returning to his ranch in Texas, the doughty ex-Senator found he was unable to retire when the Governor who had defeated him two years previously was threatening to lead the state into secession. So in the fall of 1859, the aging warrior again ran as an independent candidate for Governor, again with no party, no newspaper and no organization behind him, and making but one campaign speech. He would rely, he told his audience in that still fascinating voice, "upon the Constitution and the Union, all the old Jacksonian democracy I ever professed or officially practiced. . . . In politics I am an old fogy, because I cling devotedly to those primitive principles upon which our government was founded."

Although his opponents repeatedly insisted that secession and reopening the Texas slave trade were not real issues, Houston pressed hard on these grounds, as well as his promises of greater protection against Mexican and Indian frontier terrorisms. It was a bitter campaign, the Democrats and newspapers assailing Houston with acrimonious passion, reopening old charges of Houston's immorality and cowardice. But strangely enough, the appeal of the issues (however premature) he had raised, his personal following among his old comrades, disgust with the administration of his opponents, new popularity which Houston had acquired just prior to his retirement by his exposure on the Senate floor of a corrupt federal judge, and a surge of sentimental feeling toward him upon his return to his beloved Texas, all combined to elect Sam Houston Governor in a complete reversal of his defeat two years earlier. It was the first setback for Southern extremists in a decade, and the Governor-elect was attacked by disgusted Texas newspapers as "a traitor who ought to fall never to rise again" and "one of the greatest enemies to the South—a Southern Free Soiler."

The old Jacksonian nationalism which had motivated his entire career now faced its severest trial. Maintaining that the overwhelmingly hostile Democratic Legislature did not truly represent the people, Governor Houston violated all precedent by delivering his inaugural address directly to the people from the steps of the Capitol, instead of before a joint session of the Legislature. To an immense audience gathered on the Capitol grounds, Houston declared that he was Governor of the people and not of any party, and that "When Texas united her destiny with that of the United States, she entered not into the North or South; her connection was not sectional, but national."

But the wounds of his election were not healed; and when the name of Sam Houston was proposed by a New Yorker at the Democratic National Convention in 1860 as one that "would sweep the whole country for a great victory," ex-Governor Runnels, the leader of the Texas delegation, jumped to his feet. "Sir, by God! I am the individual Sam Houston recently thrashed for Governor and anything laudatory to him is damned unpleasant to me."

With obvious reference to such enemies, Houston told the Legislature in his first general message in 1860:

> notwithstanding the ravings of deluded zealots, or the impious threats of fanatical disunionists, the love of our common country still burns with the fire of the olden time . . . in the hearts of the conservative people of Texas. . . . Texas will maintain the Constitution and stand by the Union. It is all that can save us as a nation. Destroy it, and anarchy awaits us.

When South Carolina invited Texas to send delegates to the Southern Convention to protest "assaults upon the institution of slavery and upon the rights of the South,"

Houston transmitted the communication to the Legislature as a matter of courtesy, but warned in a masterful document: "The Union was intended to be a perpetuity." By skillful political maneuvers, he prevented acceptance of South Carolina's invitation, causing Senator Iverson of Georgia to call for some "Texan Brutus" to "rise and rid his country of the hoary-headed incubus." As sentiment grew overwhelmingly in favor of secession during the heated Presidential campaign of 1860, Governor Houston could only implore his impatient constituents to wait and see what Mr. Lincoln's attitude would be, if elected. But the fact that he had received a few unsolicited votes in the Republican Convention as Lincoln's running mate furnished further ammunition to his enemies. And when the town of Henderson mysteriously burned in August, the Governor could do nothing to prevent the wave of lynchings, vigilante committees and angry sentiment which followed rumors of Negro uprisings and arson. Houston's speech in Waco denouncing secession was answered by the explosion of a keg of powder behind the hotel in which he slept unharmed. But heedless of personal or political danger, he arose from a sickbed in September to make one final appeal:

> I ask not the defeat of sectionalism by sectionalism, but by nationality. . . . These are no new sentiments to me. I uttered them in the American Senate in 1856. I utter them now. I was denounced then as a traitor. I am denounced now. Be it so! Men who never endured the privation, the toil, the peril that I have for my country call me a traitor because I am willing to yield obedience to the Constitution and the constituted authorities. Let them suffer what I have for this Union, and they will feel it entwining so closely around their hearts that it will be like snapping the cords of life to give it up. . . . What are the people who call me a traitor? Are they those who march under the national flag and are ready to defend it? That is my banner! . . . and so long as it waves proudly o'er me, even as it has waved amid stormy scenes where these men were not, I can forget that I am called a traitor.

Abraham Lincoln was elected President, and immediately throughout Texas the Lone Star flag was hoisted in an atmosphere of excited and belligerent expectation. Houston's plea that Texas fight for her rights "in the Union and for the sake of the Union" fell on deaf ears. "A sentiment of servility," snapped the press; and Governor Houston was shoved aside as a Secession Convention was called.

Sam Houston, fighting desperately to hold on to the reins of government, called a special session of the State Legislature, denouncing extremists both North and South and insisting that he had "not yet lost the hope that our rights can be maintained in the Union." If not, he maintained, independence is preferable to joining the Southern camp.

But the Secession Convention leaders, recognized by the Legislature and aided by the desertion of the Union commander in Texas, could not be stopped, and their headlong rush into secession was momentarily disturbed only by the surprise appearance of the Governor they hated but feared. On the day the Ordinance of Secession was to be adopted, Sam Houston sat on the platform, grimly silent, his presence renewing the courage of those few friends of Union who remained in the hall. "To those who tell of his wonderful charge up the hill at San Jacinto," said the historian Wharton, "I say it took a thousand times more courage when he stalked into the Secession Convention at Austin and alone defied and awed them." When, encouraged by the magic of Houston's presence, James W. Throckmorton cast one of the seven votes against secession, he was loudly and bitterly hissed; and rising in his place he made the memorable reply, "When the rabble hiss, well may patriots tremble."

But there were few who trembled as the Ordinance was adopted and submitted to the people for their approval at the polls one month later. Immediately the fighting ex-Senator took the stump in a one-man campaign to keep Texas in the Union. Ugly crowds, stones and denunciation as a traitor met him throughout the state. At Waco his life was threatened. At Belton, an armed thug suddenly arose and started toward him. But old Sam Houston, looking him right in the eye, put each hand on his own pistols: "Ladies and Gentlemen, keep your seats. It is nothing but a fice barking at the lion in his den." Unharmed, he stalked the state in characteristic fashion, confounding his enemies with powerful sarcasm. Asked to express his honest opinion of the secessionist leader, Houston replied: "He has all the characteristics of a dog except fidelity." Now seventy years old, but still an impressively straight figure with those penetrating eyes and massive white hair, Old Sam closed his tour in Galveston before a jeering and ugly mob. "Some of you laugh to scorn the idea of bloodshed as the result of secession," he cried, "but let me tell you what is coming. You may, after the sacrifice of countless millions of treasures and hundreds of thousands of precious lives, as a bare possibility, win Southern independence, if God be not against you. But I doubt it. The North is determined to preserve this Union."

His prophecy was unheeded. On February 23, Texas voted for secession by a large margin: and on March 2, the anniversary of Houston's birthday and Texan independence, the special convention reassembled at Austin and declared that Texas had seceded. Governor Houston, still desperately attempting to regain the initiative, indicated he would make known his plans on the matter to the legislature. Angry at his insistence that its legal authority had ended, the Convention by a thumping vote of 109 to 2 declared Texas to be a part of the Southern Confederacy, and decreed that all state officers must take the new oath of allegiance on the fourteenth of March. The Governor's secretary merely replied that Governor Houston "did not acknowledge the existence of the

Convention and should not regard its action as binding upon him."

On March 14, as an eyewitness described it, the Convention hall was "crowded . . . electrified with fiery radiations, of men tingling with passion, and glowing and burning with the anticipation of revengeful battle. The air was full of the stirring clamor of a multitude of voices—angry, triumphant, scornful with an occasional oath or epithet of contempt—but the voice of Sam Houston was not heard."

At the appointed hour, the Convention clerk was instructed to call the roll of state officials. Silence settled over the vast audience, and every eye peered anxiously for a glimpse of the old hero.

"Sam Houston!" There was no response.

"Sam Houston! Sam Houston!" The rumbling and contemptuous voices began again. The office of Governor of Texas, Confederate States of America, was declared to be officially vacant; and Lieutenant Governor Edward Clark, "an insignificant creature, contemptible, spry and pert," stepped up to take the oath. (A close personal and political friend elected on Houston's ticket, Clark would later enter the executive office to demand the archives of the state, only to have his former mentor wheel slowly in his chair to face him with the grandly scornful question: "And what is your name, sir?")

In another part of the Capitol, the hero of San Jacinto, casting aside a lifetime of political fortune, fame and devotion from his people, was scrawling out his last message as Governor with a broken heart:

> Fellow Citizens, in the name of your rights and liberty, which I believe have been trampled upon, I refuse to take this oath. In the name of my own conscience and my own manhood . . . I refuse to take this oath. . . . [But] I love Texas too well to bring civil strife and bloodshed upon her. I shall make no endeavor to maintain my authority as Chief

Executive of this state, except by the peaceful exercise of my functions. When I can no longer do this, I shall calmly withdraw from the scene. . . . I am . . . stricken down because I will not yield those principles which I have fought for. . . . The severest pang is that the blow comes in the name of the state of Texas.

PART THREE

The Time and the Place

The end of the costly military struggle between North and South did not restore peace and unity on the political front. Appomattox had ended the shooting of brother by brother; but it did not halt the political invasions, the economic plundering and the intersectional hatred that still racked a divided land. The bitter animosities on both sides of the Mason-Dixon line which had engulfed Daniel Webster, Thomas Hart Benton and Sam Houston continued unabated for some two decades after the war. Those in the North who sought to bind up the wounds of the nation and treat the South with mercy and fairness—men like President Andrew Johnson, and those Senators who stood by him in his impeachment—were pilloried for their lack of patriotism by those who waved the "bloody shirt." Those in the South who sought to demonstrate to the nation that the fanatical sectionalism of their region had been forgotten—men like Lucius Quintus Cincinnatus Lamar of Mississippi—were attacked by their constituents as deserters to the conquering enemy. When Confederate General Bob Toombs was asked why he did not petition Congress for his pardon, Toombs replied with quiet grandeur: "Pardon for what? I have not yet pardoned the North."

But gradually, the old conflicts over emancipation and reconstruction faded away, and exploitation of the newly opened West and the trampled South brought new issues and new faces to the Senate. It was no longer the forum for our greatest Constitutional lawyers, for Constitutional issues no longer dominated American public life. Easy money, sudden fortunes, increasingly powerful political machines and blatant corruption transformed much of the nation; and the Senate, as befits a democratic legislative body, accurately represented the nation. Corporation lawyers and political bosses, not constitutional orators, were the spokesmen for this roaring era; although too many of the nation's talented men found fame and fortune more readily available in the world of high finance and industry, rather than the seemingly dull and unnoticed labors of government. (If Daniel Webster had lived in that age, one editor commented, he would have been "neither in debt nor in the Senate.") Eleven new states were added quickly as the West was developed; and twenty-two new Senators and a tremendous new chamber detracted from that old distinctive atmosphere. Sectionalism, logrolling and a series of near-fanatical movements—of which the "free silver" movement that embroiled Lamar was only the beginning—plagued Senate deliberations on domestic economic issues. "We are becoming a mere collection of local potato plots and cabbage grounds," complained one Senator, weary of the constant bickering over local patronage, rivers and harbors projects and tariff-protected industries.

Senators, said William Allen White, represented not only states and regions but "principalities and powers and business":

> One Senator, for instance, represented the Union Pacific Railway System, another the New York Central, still an-

other the insurance interests. . . . Coal and iron owned a coterie . . . cotton had half a dozen Senators. And so it went. . . . It was a plutocratic feudalism . . . eminently respectable. The collar of any great financial interest was worn in pride.

And White related the supposed conversation in which veteran Senator Davis described to a freshman Senator the characteristics of his colleagues in those roaring days as they came down the aisle: "The jackal; the vulture; the sheep-killing dog; the gorilla; the crocodile; the buzzard; the old clucking hen; the dove; the turkey-gobbler." Then, White wrote, "as the big hulk of a greedy westerner—coarse, devious, insolent—came swinging in heavily, Judge Davis pointed his stubby forefinger at the creature and exclaimed: 'A wolf, sir; a damned, hungry, skulking, cowardly wolf!' "

Thus by the end of the nineteenth century the Senate had come to very nearly its lowest ebb, in terms of power as well as prestige. The decline in Senatorial power had begun shortly after the end of Grant's administration. Prior to that time, the Senate, which had humiliated President Johnson and dominated President Grant, had reigned supreme in what was very nearly a parliamentary form of government. Senators even claimed a place at the dinner table above members of the Cabinet (who had previously outranked them at social functions). "If they visited the White House," George Frisbie Hoar later recalled, "it was to give, not to receive advice." (Indeed the assertion of power by both Houses was illustrated by the visit of Congressman Anson Burlingame to the House of Commons. When an attendant told him he must leave his seat, inasmuch as that particular gallery was reserved for Peers, an old Peer sitting nearby interposed. "Let him stay, let him stay. He is a Peer in his own country." "I am a Sovereign in my own country, Sir," replied the Congressman as he walked out, "and shall lose caste if I associate with Peers.") But the peak of Congressional power passed as Presidents Hayes, Garfield, Arthur and Cleveland successfully resisted Senatorial attempts to dictate Presidential appointments, and the government returned to the more traditional American system of the Constitution's checks and balances.

The decline in the Senate's power, moreover, had been foreshadowed by a rapid decline in prestige even before economic issues had replaced the sectional and constitutional conflict. British and Canadian diplomats maintained that they had secured approval of the Reciprocity Treaty of 1854 by seeing to it that it was "floated through on waves of champagne. . . . If you have got to deal with hogs, what are you to do?" A Cabinet member, possibly recalling this metaphor, impatiently told Henry Adams in 1869, "You can't use tact with a Congressman! A Congressman is a hog! You must take a stick and hit him on the snout." And in quiet derision Adams, who thought most members of the Senate "more grotesque than ridicule could make them," had replied, "If a Congressman is a hog, what is a Senator?"

But the Senate, despite its decline in power and public esteem during the second half of the nineteenth century, did not consist entirely of hogs and damned skulking wolves. It still contained men worthy of respect, and men of courage. Of these, Edmund Ross and those who stood with him in the Johnson impeachment trial selflessly sacrificed themselves to save the nation from reckless abuse of legislative power. And Lucius Lamar, by his gentle but firm determination to be a statesman, was instrumental in reuniting the nation in preparation for the new challenges which lay ahead.

VI

EDMUND G. ROSS

"I . . . LOOKED DOWN INTO MY OPEN GRAVE."

In a lonely grave, forgotten and unknown, lies "the man who saved a President," and who as a result may well have preserved for ourselves and posterity constitutional government in the United States—the man who performed in 1868 what one historian has called "the most heroic act in American history, incomparably more difficult than any deed of valor upon the field of battle" —but a United States Senator whose name no one recalls: Edmund G. Ross of Kansas.

The impeachment of President Andrew Johnson, the event in which the obscure Ross was to play such a dramatic role, was the sensational climax to the bitter struggle between the President, determined to carry out Abraham Lincoln's policies of reconciliation with the defeated South, and the more radical Republican leaders in Congress, who sought to administer the downtrodden Southern states as conquered provinces which had forfeited their rights under the Constitution. It was, moreover, a struggle between Executive and Legislative authority. Andrew Johnson, the courageous if untactful

Tennessean who had been the only Southern Member of Congress to refuse to secede with his state, had committed himself to the policies of the Great Emancipator to whose high station he had succeeded only by the course of an assassin's bullet. He knew that Lincoln prior to his death had already clashed with the extremists in Congress, who had opposed his approach to reconstruction in a constitutional and charitable manner and sought to make the Legislative Branch of the government supreme. And his own belligerent temperament soon destroyed any hope that Congress might now join hands in carrying out Lincoln's policies of permitting the South to resume its place in the Union with as little delay and controversy as possible.

By 1866, when Edmund Ross first came to the Senate, the two branches of the government were already at each other's throats, snarling and bristling with anger. Bill after bill was vetoed by the President on the grounds that they were unconstitutional, too harsh in their treatment of the South, an unnecessary prolongation of military rule in peacetime or undue interference with the authority of the Executive Branch. And for the first time in our nation's history, important public measures were passed over a President's veto and became law without his support.

But not all of Andrew Johnson's vetoes were overturned; and the "Radical" Republicans of the Congress promptly realized that one final step was necessary before they could crush their despised foe (and in the heat of political battle their vengeance was turned upon their President far more than their former military enemies of the South). That one remaining step was the assurance of a two-thirds majority in the Senate—for under the Constitution, such a majority was necessary to override a Presidential veto. And more important, such a majority was constitutionally required to accomplish their major ambition, now an ill-kept secret, conviction of the President under an impeachment and his dismissal from office!

The temporary and unstable two-thirds majority which had enabled the Senate Radical Republicans on several occasions to enact legislation over the President's veto was, they knew, insufficiently reliable for an impeachment conviction. To solidify this bloc became the paramount goal of Congress, expressly or impliedly governing its decisions on other issues—particularly the admission of new states, the readmission of Southern states and the determination of senatorial credentials. By extremely dubious methods a pro-Johnson Senator was denied his seat. Over the President's veto Nebraska was admitted to the Union, seating two more anti-administration Senators. Although last-minute maneuvers failed to admit Colorado over the President's veto (sparsely populated Colorado had rejected statehood in a referendum), an unexpected tragedy brought false tears and fresh hopes for a new vote, in Kansas.

Senator Jim Lane of Kansas had been a "conservative" Republican sympathetic to Johnson's plans to carry out Lincoln's reconstruction policies. But his frontier state was one of the most "radical" in the Union. When Lane voted to uphold Johnson's veto of the Civil Rights Bill of 1866 and introduced the administration's bill for recognition of the new state government of Arkansas, Kansas had arisen in outraged heat. A mass meeting at Lawrence had vilified the Senator and speedily reported resolutions sharply condemning his position. Humiliated, mentally ailing, broken in health and laboring under charges of financial irregularities, Jim Lane took his own life on July 1, 1866.

With this thorn in their side removed, the Radical Republicans in Washington looked anxiously toward Kansas and the selection of Lane's successor. Their fondest hopes were realized, for the new Senator from Kansas turned out to be Edmund G. Ross, the very man who had introduced the resolutions attacking Lane at Lawrence.

There could be no doubt as to where Ross's sympathies lay, for his entire career was one of determined opposition to the slave states of the South, their practices and their friends. In 1854, when only twenty-eight, he had taken part in the mob rescue of a fugitive slave in Milwaukee. In 1856, he had joined that flood of antislavery immigrants to "bleeding" Kansas who intended to keep it a free territory. Disgusted with the Democratic party of his youth, he had left that party, and volunteered in the Kansas Free State Army to drive back a force of proslavery men invading the territory. In 1862, he had given up his newspaper work to enlist in the Union Army, from which he emerged a Major. His leading role in the condemnation of Lane at Lawrence convinced the Radical Republican leaders in Congress that in Edmund G. Ross they had a solid member of that vital two-thirds.

The stage was now set for the final scene—the removal of Johnson. Early in 1867, Congress enacted over the President's veto the Tenure-of-Office Bill which prevented the President from removing without the consent of the Senate all new officeholders whose appointment required confirmation by that body. At the time nothing more than the cry for more patronage was involved, Cabinet Members having originally been specifically exempt.

On August 5, 1867, President Johnson—convinced that the Secretary of War, whom he had inherited from Lincoln, Edwin M. Stanton, was the surreptitious tool of the Radical Republicans and was seeking to become the almighty dictator of the conquered South—asked for his immediate resignation; and Stanton arrogantly fired back the reply that he declined to resign before the next meeting of Congress. Not one to cower before this kind of effrontery, the President one week later suspended Stanton, and appointed in his place the one man whom Stanton did not dare resist, General Grant. On January 13, 1868, an angry Senate notified the President and Grant that it did not concur in the suspension of Stanton, and Grant vacated the office upon Stanton's return. But the situation was intolerable. The Secretary of War was unable to attend Cabinet meetings or associate with his colleagues in the administration; and on February 21, President Johnson, anxious to obtain a court test of the act he believed obviously unconstitutional, again notified Stanton that he had been summarily removed from the office of Secretary of War.

While Stanton, refusing to yield possession, barricaded himself in his office, public opinion in the nation ran heavily against the President. He had intentionally broken the law and dictatorially thwarted the will of Congress! Although previous resolutions of impeachment had been defeated in the House, both in committee and on the floor, a new resolution was swiftly reported and adopted on February 24 by a tremendous vote. Every single Republican voted in the affirmative, and Thaddeus Stevens of Pennsylvania—the crippled, fanatical personification of the extremes of the Radical Republican movement, master of the House of Representatives, with a mouth like the thin edge of an ax—warned both Houses of the Congress coldly: "Let me see the recreant who would vote to let such a criminal escape. Point me to one who will dare do it and I will show you one who will dare the infamy of posterity."

With the President impeached—in effect, indicted—by the House, the frenzied trial for his conviction or acquittal under the Articles of Impeachment began on March 5 in the Senate, presided over by the Chief Justice. It was a trial to rank with all the great trials in history—Charles I before the High Court of Justice, Louis XVI before the French Convention, and Warren Hastings before the House of Lords. Two great elements of drama were missing: the actual cause for which the President was being tried was not fundamental to the welfare of the nation; and the defendant himself was at all times absent.

But every other element of the highest courtroom drama was present. To each Senator the Chief Justice administered an oath "to do impartial justice" (including even the hot-headed Radical Senator from Ohio, Benjamin Wade, who as President Pro Tempore of the Senate was next in line for the Presidency). The chief prosecutor for the House was General Benjamin F. Butler, the "butcher of New Orleans," a talented but coarse and demagogic Congressman from Massachusetts. (When he lost his seat in 1874, he was so hated by his own party as well as his opponents that one Republican wired concerning the Democratic sweep, "Butler defeated, everything else lost.") Some one thousand tickets were printed for admission to the Senate galleries during the trial, and every conceivable device was used to obtain one of the four tickets allotted each Senator.

From the fifth of March to the sixteenth of May, the drama continued. Of the eleven Articles of Impeachment adopted by the House, the first eight were based upon the removal of Stanton and the appointment of a new Secretary of War in violation of the Tenure-of-Office Act; the ninth related to Johnson's conversation with a general which was said to induce violations of the Army Appropriations Act; the tenth recited that Johnson had delivered "intemperate, inflammatory and scandalous harangues . . . as well against Congress as the laws of the United States"; and the eleventh was a deliberately obscure conglomeration of all the charges in the preceding articles, which had been designed by Thaddeus Stevens to furnish a common ground for those who favored conviction but were unwilling to identify themselves on basic issues. In opposition to Butler's inflammatory arguments in support of this hastily drawn indictment, Johnson's able and learned counsel replied with considerable effectiveness. They insisted that the Tenure-of-Office Act was null and void as a clear violation of the Constitution; that even if it were valid, it would not apply to Stanton, for the reasons previously mentioned; and that the only way that a judicial test of the law could be obtained was for Stanton to be dismissed and sue for his rights in the courts.

But as the trial progressed, it became increasingly apparent that the impatient Republicans did not intend to give the President a fair trial on the formal issues upon which the impeachment was drawn, but intended instead to depose him from the White House on any grounds, real or imagined, for refusing to accept their policies. Telling evidence in the President's favor was arbitrarily excluded. Prejudgment on the part of most Senators was brazenly announced. Attempted bribery and other forms of pressure were rampant. The chief interest was not in the trial or the evidence, but in the tallying of votes necessary for conviction.

Twenty-seven states (excluding the unrecognized Southern states) in the Union meant fifty-four members of the Senate, and thirty-six votes were required to constitute the two-thirds majority necessary for conviction. All twelve Democratic votes were obviously lost, and the forty-two Republicans knew that they could afford to lose only six of their own members if Johnson were to be ousted. To their dismay, at a preliminary Republican caucus, six courageous Republicans indicated that the evidence so far introduced was not in their opinion sufficient to convict Johnson under the Articles of Impeachment. "Infamy!" cried the Philadelphia *Press.* The Republic has "been betrayed in the house of its friends!"

But if the remaining thirty-six Republicans would

hold, there would be no doubt as to the outcome. All must stand together! But one Republican Senator would not announce his verdict in the preliminary poll—Edmund G. Ross of Kansas. The Radicals were outraged that a Senator from such an anti-Johnson stronghold as Kansas could be doubtful. "It was a very clear case," Senator Sumner of Massachusetts fumed, "especially for a Kansas man. I did not think that a Kansas man could quibble against his country."

From the very time Ross had taken his seat, the Radical leaders had been confident of his vote. His entire background, as already indicated, was one of firm support of their cause. One of his first acts in the Senate had been to read a declaration of his adherence to Radical Republican policy, and he had silently voted for all of their measures. He had made it clear that he was not in sympathy with Andrew Johnson personally or politically; and after the removal of Stanton, he had voted with the majority in adopting a resolution declaring such removal unlawful. His colleague from Kansas, Senator Pomeroy, was one of the most Radical leaders of the anti-Johnson group. The Republicans insisted that Ross's crucial vote was rightfully theirs, and they were determined to get it by whatever means available. As stated by De Witt in his memorable *Impeachment of Andrew Johnson*, "The full brunt of the struggle turned at last on the one remaining doubtful Senator, Edmund G. Ross."

When the impeachment resolution had passed the House, Senator Ross had casually remarked to Senator Sprague of Rhode Island, "Well, Sprague, the thing is here; and, so far as I am concerned, though a Republican and opposed to Mr. Johnson and his policy, he shall have as fair a trial as an accused man ever had on this earth." Immediately the word spread that "Ross was shaky." "From that hour," he later wrote, "not a day passed that did not bring me, by mail and telegraph and in personal intercourse, appeals to stand fast for impeachment, and not a few were the admonitions of condign visitations upon any indication even of lukewarmness."

Throughout the country, and in all walks of life, as indicated by the correspondence of Members of the Senate, the condition of the public mind was not unlike that preceding a great battle. The dominant party of the nation seemed to occupy the position of public prosecutor, and it was scarcely in the mood to brook delay for trial or to hear defense. Washington had become during the trial the central point of the politically dissatisfied and swarmed with representatives of every state of the Union, demanding in a practically united voice the deposition of the President. The footsteps of the anti-impeaching Republicans were dogged from the day's beginning to its end and far into the night, with entreaties, considerations, and threats. The newspapers came daily filled with not a few threats of violence upon their return to their constituents.

Ross and his fellow doubtful Republicans were daily pestered, spied upon and subjected to every form of pressure. Their residences were carefully watched, their social circles suspiciously scrutinized, and their every move and companions secretly marked in special notebooks. They were warned in the party press, harangued by their constituents, and sent dire warnings threatening political ostracism and even assassination. Stanton himself, from his barricaded headquarters in the War Department, worked day and night to bring to bear upon the doubtful Senators all the weight of his impressive military associations. The Philadelphia *Press* reported "a fearful avalanche of telegrams from every section of the country," a great surge of public opinion from the "common people" who had given their money and lives to the country and would not "willingly or unavenged see their great sacrifice made naught."

The New York *Tribune* reported that Edmund Ross in particular was "mercilessly dragged this way and that by both sides, hunted like a fox night and day and badgered by his own colleagues, like the bridge at Arcola now trod upon by one Army and now trampled by the other." His background and life were investigated from top to bottom, and his constituents and colleagues pursued him throughout Washington to gain some inkling of his opinion. He was the target of every eye, his name was on every mouth and his intentions were discussed in every newspaper. Although there is evidence that he gave some hint of agreement to each side, and each attempted to claim him publicly, he actually kept both sides in a state of complete suspense by his judicial silence.

But with no experience in political turmoil, no reputation in the Senate, no independent income and the most radical state in the Union to deal with, Ross was judged to be the most sensitive to criticism and the most certain to be swayed by expert tactics. A committee of Congressmen and Senators sent to Kansas, and to the states of the other doubtful Republicans, this telegram: "Great danger to the peace of the country and the Republican cause if impeachment fails. Send to your Senators public opinion by resolutions, letters, and delegations." A member of the Kansas Legislature called upon Ross at the Capitol. A general urged on by Stanton remained at his lodge until four o'clock in the morning determined to see him. His brother received a letter offering $20,000 for revelation of the Senator's intentions. Gruff Ben Butler exclaimed of Ross, "There is a bushel of money! How much does the damned scoundrel want?" The night before the Senate was to take its first vote for the conviction or acquittal of Johnson, Ross received this telegram from home:

> Kansas has heard the evidence and demands the conviction of the President.
>
> (*signed*) D. R. ANTHONY AND 1,000 OTHERS

And on that fateful morning of May 16 Ross replied:

> To D. R. Anthony and 1,000 Others: I do not recognize your right to demand that I vote either for or against con-

viction. I have taken an oath to do impartial justice according to the Constitution and laws, and trust that I shall have the courage to vote according to the dictates of my judgment and for the highest good of the country.

[signed]—E. G. Ross

That morning spies traced Ross to his breakfast; and ten minutes before the vote was taken his Kansas colleague warned him in the presence of Thaddeus Stevens that a vote for acquittal would mean trumped-up charges and his political death.

But now the fateful hour was at hand. Neither escape, delay or indecision was possible. As Ross himself later described it: "The galleries were packed. Tickets of admission were at an enormous premium. The House had adjourned and all of its members were in the Senate chamber. Every chair on the Senate floor was filled with a Senator, a Cabinet Officer, a member of the President's counsel or a member of the House." Every Senator was in his seat, the desperately ill Grimes of Iowa being literally carried in.

It had been decided to take the first vote under that broad Eleventh Article of Impeachment, believed to command the widest support. As the Chief Justice announced the voting would begin, he reminded "the citizens and strangers in the galleries that absolute silence and perfect order are required." But already a deathlike stillness enveloped the Senate chamber. A Congressman later recalled that "Some of the members of the House near me grew pale and sick under the burden of suspense"; and Ross noted that there was even "a subsidence of the shuffling of feet, the rustling of silks, the fluttering of fans, and of conversation."

The voting tensely commenced. By the time the Chief Justice reached the name of Edmund Ross twenty-four "guilties" had been pronounced. Ten more were certain and one other practically certain. Only Ross's vote was needed to obtain the thirty-six votes necessary to convict the President. But not a single person in the room knew how this young Kansan would vote. Unable to conceal the suspense and emotion in his voice, the Chief Justice put the question to him: "Mr. Senator Ross, how say you? Is the respondent Andrew Johnson guilty or not guilty of a high misdemeanor as charged in this Article?" Every voice was still; every eye was upon the freshman Senator from Kansas. The hopes and fears, the hatred and bitterness of past decades were centered upon this one man.

As Ross himself later described it, his "powers of hearing and seeing seemed developed in an abnormal degree."

> Every individual in that great audience seemed distinctly visible, some with lips apart and bending forward in anxious expectancy, others with hand uplifted as if to ward off an apprehended blow . . . and each peering with an intensity that was almost tragic upon the face of him who was about to cast the fateful vote. . . . Every fan was folded, not a foot moved, not the rustle of a garment, not a whisper was heard. . . . Hope and fear seemed blended in every face, instantaneously alternating, some with revengeful hate . . . others lighted with hope. . . . The Senators in their seats leaned over their desks, many with hand to ear. . . . It was a tremendous responsibility, and it was not strange that he upon whom it had been imposed by a fateful combination of conditions should have sought to avoid it, to put it away from him as one shuns, or tries to fight off, a nightmare. . . . I almost literally looked down into my open grave. Friendships, position, fortune, everything that makes life desirable to an ambitious man were about to be swept away by the breath of my mouth, perhaps forever. It is not strange that my answer was carried waveringly over the air and failed to reach the limits of the audience, or that repetition was called for by distant Senators on the opposite side of the Chamber.

Then came the answer again in a voice that could not be misunderstood—full, final, definite, unhesitating and unmistakable: "Not guilty." The deed was done, the President saved, the trial as good as over and the conviction lost. The remainder of the roll call was unimportant; conviction had failed by the margin of a single vote and a general rumbling filled the chamber until the Chief Justice proclaimed that "on this Article thirty-five Senators having voted guilty and nineteen not guilty, a two-thirds majority not having voted for conviction, the President is, therefore, acquitted under this Article."

A ten-day recess followed, ten turbulent days to change votes on the remaining Articles. An attempt was made to rush through bills to readmit six Southern states, whose twelve Senators were guaranteed to vote for conviction. But this could not be accomplished in time. Again Ross was the only one uncommitted on the other Articles, the only one whose vote could not be predicted in advance. And again he was subjected to terrible pressure. From "D. R. Anthony and others," he received a wire informing him that "Kansas repudiates you as she does all perjurers and skunks." Every incident in his life was examined and distorted. Professional witnesses were found by Senator Pomeroy to testify before a special House committee that Ross had indicated a willingness to change his vote for a consideration. (Unfortunately this witness was so delighted in his exciting role that he also swore that Senator Pomeroy had made an offer to produce three votes for acquittal for $40,000.) When Ross, in his capacity as a Committee Chairman, took several bills to the President, James G. Blaine remarked: "There goes the rascal to get his pay." (Long afterward Blaine was to admit: "In the exaggerated denunciation caused by the anger and chagrin of the moment, great injustice was done to statesmen of spotless character.")

Again the wild rumors spread that Ross had been won over on the remaining Articles of Impeachment. As the Senate reassembled, he was the only one of the seven "renegade" Republicans to vote with the majority on preliminary procedural matters. But when the second and third Articles of Impeachment were read, and the name of Ross was reached again with the same intense suspense of ten days earlier, again came the calm answer "Not guilty."

Why did Ross, whose dislike for Johnson continued, vote "Not guilty"? His motives appear clearly from his own writings on the subject years later in articles contributed to *Scribner's* and *Forum* magazines:

> In a large sense, the independence of the executive office as a coordinate branch of the government was on trial. . . . If . . . the President must step down . . . a disgraced man and a political outcast . . . upon insufficient proofs and from partisan considerations, the office of President would be degraded, cease to be a coordinate branch of the government, and ever after subordinated to the legislative will. It would practically have revolutionized our splendid political fabric into a partisan Congressional autocracy. . . . This government had never faced so insidious a danger . . . control by the worst element of American politics. . . . If Andrew Johnson were acquitted by a nonpartisan vote . . . America would pass the danger point of partisan rule and that intolerance which so often characterizes the sway of great majorities and makes them dangerous.

The "open grave" which Edmund Ross had foreseen was hardly an exaggeration. A Justice of the Kansas Supreme Court telegraphed him that "the rope with which Judas Iscariot hanged himself is lost, but Jim Lane's pistol is at your service." An editorial in a Kansas newspaper screamed:

> On Saturday last Edmund G. Ross, United States Senator from Kansas, sold himself, and betrayed his constituents; stultified his own record, basely lied to his friends, shamefully violated his solemn pledge . . . and to the utmost of his poor ability signed the death warrant of his country's liberty. This act was done deliberately, because the traitor, like Benedict Arnold, loved money better than he did principle, friends, honor and his country, all combined. Poor, pitiful, shriveled wretch, with a soul so small that a little pelf would outweigh all things else that dignify or ennoble manhood.

Ross's political career was ended. To the New York *Tribune,* he was nothing but "a miserable poltroon and traitor." The Philadelphia *Press* said that in Ross "littleness" had "simply borne its legitimate fruit," and that he and his fellow recalcitrant Republicans had "plunged from a precipice of fame into the groveling depths of infamy and death." The Philadelphia *Inquirer* said that "They had tried, convicted and sentenced themselves." For them there could be "no allowance, no clemency."

Comparative peace returned to Washington as Stanton relinquished his office and Johnson served out the rest of his term, later—unlike his Republican defenders—to return triumphantly to the Senate as Senator from Tennessee. But no one paid attention when Ross tried unsuccessfully to explain his vote, and denounced the falsehoods of Ben Butler's investigating committee, recalling that the General's "well known grovelling instincts and proneness to slime and uncleanness" had led "the public to insult the brute creation by dubbing him 'the beast.'" He clung unhappily to his seat in the Senate until the expiration of his term, frequently referred to as "the traitor Ross," and complaining that his fellow Congressmen, as well as citizens on the street, considered association with him "disreputable and scandalous," and passed him by as if he were "a leper, with averted face and every indication of hatred and disgust."

Neither Ross nor any other Republican who had voted for the acquittal of Johnson was ever re-elected to the Senate, not a one of them retaining the support of their party's organization. When he returned to Kansas in 1871, he and his family suffered social ostracism, physical attack, and near poverty.

Who was Edmund G. Ross? Practically nobody. Not a single public law bears his name, not a single history book includes his picture, not a single list of Senate "greats" mentions his service. His one heroic deed has been all but forgotten. But who might Edmund G. Ross have been? That is the question—for Ross, a man with an excellent command of words, an excellent background for politics and an excellent future in the Senate, might well have outstripped his colleagues in prestige and power throughout a long Senate career. Instead, he chose to throw all of this away for one act of conscience.

But the twisting course of human events eventually upheld the faith he expressed to his wife shortly after the trial: "Millions of men cursing me today will bless me tomorrow for having saved the country from the greatest peril through which it has ever passed, though none but God can ever know the struggle it has cost me." For twenty years later Congress repealed the Tenure-of-Office Act, to which every President after Johnson, regardless of party, had objected; and still later the Supreme Court, referring to "the extremes of that episode in our government," held it to be unconstitutional. Ross moved to New Mexico, where in his later years he was to be appointed Territorial Governor. Just prior to his death when he was awarded a special pension by Congress for his service in the Civil War, the press and the country took the opportunity to pay tribute to his fidelity to principle in a trying hour and his courage in saving his government from a devastating reign of terror. They now agreed with Ross's earlier judgment that his vote had "saved the country from . . . a strain that would have wrecked any other form of government." Those Kansas newspapers and political leaders who had bitterly denounced him in earlier years praised Ross for his stand against legislative mob rule: "By the firmness and courage of Senator Ross," it was said, "the country was saved from calamity greater than war, while it consigned him to a political martyrdom, the most cruel in our history. . . . Ross was the victim of a wild flame of intolerance which swept everything before it. He did his duty knowing that it meant his political death. . . . It was a brave thing for Ross to do, but Ross did it. He acted for his conscience and with a lofty patriotism, regardless of what he knew must be the ruinous consequences to himself. He acted right."

* * *

I could not close the story of Edmund Ross without some more adequate mention of those six courageous Republicans who stood with Ross and braved denunciation to acquit Andrew Johnson. Edmund Ross, more than any of those six colleagues, endured more before and after his vote, reached his conscientious decision with greater difficulty, and aroused the greatest interest and suspense prior to May 16 by his noncommittal silence. His story, like his vote, is the key to the impeachment tragedy. But all seven of the Republicans who voted against conviction should be remembered for their courage. Not a single one of them ever won re-election to the Senate. Not a single one of them escaped the unholy combination of threats, bribes and coercive tactics by which their fellow Republicans attempted to intimidate their votes; and not a single one of them escaped the terrible torture of vicious criticism engendered by their vote to acquit.

William Pitt Fessenden of Maine, one of the most eminent Senators, orators and lawyers of his day, and a prominent senior Republican leader, who admired Stanton and disliked Johnson, became convinced early in the game that "the whole thing is a mere madness."

> The country has so bad an opinion of the President, which he fully deserves, that it expects his condemnation. Whatever may be the consequences to myself personally, whatever I may think and feel as a politician, I will not decide the question against my own judgment. I would rather be confined to planting cabbages the remainder of my days. . . . Make up your mind, if need be, to hear me denounced a traitor and perhaps hanged in effigy. All imaginable abuse

has been heaped upon me by the men and papers devoted to the impeachers. I have received several letters from friends warning me that my political grave is dug if I do not vote for conviction, and several threatening assassination. It is rather hard at my time of life, after a long career, to find myself the target of pointed arrows from those whom I have faithfully served. The public, when aroused and excited by passion and prejudice, is little better than a wild beast. I shall at all events retain my own self-respect and a clear conscience, and time will do justice to my motives at least.

The Radical Republicans were determined to win over the respected Fessenden, whose name would be the first question mark on the call of the roll, and his mail from Maine was abusive, threatening and pleading. Wendell Phillips scornfully told a hissing crowd that "it takes six months for a statesmanlike idea to find its way into Mr. Fessenden's head. I don't say he is lacking; he is only very slow."

Fessenden decided to shun all newspapers and screen his mail. But when one of his oldest political friends in Maine urged him to "hang Johnson up by the heels like a dead crow in a cornfield, to frighten all of his tribe," noting that he was "sure I express the unanimous feeling of every loyal heart and head in this state," Fessenden indignantly replied:

> I am acting as a judge . . . by what right can any man upon whom no responsibility rests, and who does not even hear the evidence, undertake to advise me as to what the judgment, and even the sentence, should be? I wish all my friends and constituents to understand that I, and not they, am sitting in judgment upon the President. I, not they, have sworn to do impartial justice. I, not they, am responsible to God and man for my action and its consequences.

On that tragic afternoon of May 16, as Ross described it, Senator Fessenden "was in his place, pale and haggard, yet ready for the political martyrdom which he was about to face, and which not long afterward drove him to his grave."

The first Republican Senator to ring out "Not guilty" —and the first of the seven to go to his grave, hounded by the merciless abuse that had dimmed all hope for re-election—was William Pitt Fessenden of Maine.

John B. Henderson of Missouri, one of the Senate's youngest members, had previously demonstrated high courage by introducing the Thirteenth Amendment abolishing slavery, simply because he was convinced that it would pass only if sponsored by a slave-state Senator, whose political death would necessarily follow. But when the full delegation of Republican representatives from his state cornered him in his office to demand that he convict the hated Johnson, warning that Missouri Republicans could stomach no other course, Henderson's usual courage wavered. He meekly offered to wire his resignation to the Governor, enabling a new appointee to vote for conviction; and, when it was doubted whether a new Senator would be permitted to vote, he agreed to ascertain whether his own vote would be crucial.

But an insolent and threatening telegram from Missouri restored his sense of honor, and he swiftly wired his reply: "Say to my friends that I am sworn to do impartial justice according to law and conscience, and I will try to do it like an honest man."

John Henderson voted for acquittal, the last important act of his Senatorial career. Denounced, threatened and burned in effigy in Missouri, he did not even bother to seek re-election to the Senate. Years later his party would realize its debt to him, and return him to lesser offices, but for the Senate, whose integrity he had upheld, he was through.

Peter Van Winkle of West Virginia, the last doubtful Republican name to be called on May 16, was, like Ross, a "nobody"; but his firm "Not guilty" extinguished the last faint glimmer of hope which Edmund Ross had already all but destroyed. The Republicans had counted on Van Winkle—West Virginia's first United States

Senator, and a critic of Stanton's removal; and for his courage, he was labeled "West Virginia's betrayer" by the Wheeling *Intelligencer,* who declared to the world that there was not a loyal citizen in the state who had not been misrepresented by his vote. He, too, had insured his permanent withdrawal from politics as soon as his Senate term expired.

The veteran Lyman Trumbull of Illinois, who had defeated Abe Lincoln for the Senate, had drafted much of the major reconstruction legislation which Johnson vetoed, and had voted to censure Johnson upon Stanton's removal.

But, in the eyes of the Philadelphia *Press,* his "statesmanship drivelled into selfishness," for, resisting tremendous pressure, he voted against conviction. A Republican convention in Chicago had resolved "That any Senator elected by the votes of Union Republicans, who at this time blenches and betrays, is infamous and should be dishonored and execrated while this free government endures." And an Illinois Republican leader had warned the distinguished Trumbull "not to show himself on the streets in Chicago; for I fear that the representatives of an indignant people would hang him to the most convenient lamppost."

But Lyman Trumbull, ending a brilliant career of public service and devotion to the party which would renounce him, filed for the record these enduring words:

> The question to be decided is not whether Andrew Johnson is a proper person to fill the Presidential office, nor whether it is fit that he should remain in it. . . . Once set, the example of impeaching a President for what, when the excitement of the House shall have subsided, will be regarded as insufficient cause, no future President will be safe who happens to differ with a majority of the House and two-thirds of the Senate on any measure deemed by them important. . . . What then becomes of the checks and balances of the Constitution so carefully devised and so vital to its perpetuity? They are all gone. . . . I cannot be an instru-

ment to produce such a result, and at the hazard of the ties even of friendship and affection, till calmer times shall do justice to my motives, no alternative is left me but the inflexible discharge of duty.

Joseph Smith Fowler of Tennessee, like Ross, Henderson, and Van Winkle a freshman Senator, at first thought the President impeachable. But the former Nashville professor was horrified by the mad passion of the House in rushing through the impeachment resolution by evidence against Johnson "based on falsehood," and by the "corrupt and dishonorable" Ben Butler, "a wicked man who seeks to convert the Senate of the United States into a political guillotine." He refused to be led by the nose by "politicians, thrown to the surface through the disjointed time . . . keeping alive the embers of the departing revolution." Threatened, investigated and defamed by his fellow Radical Republicans, the nervous Fowler so faltered in his reply on May 16 that it was at first mistaken for the word "guilty." A wave of triumph swept the Senate—Johnson was convicted, Ross's vote was not needed! But then came the clear and distinct answer: "Not guilty."

His re-election impossible, Fowler quietly retired from the Senate at the close of his term two years later, but not without a single statement in defense of his vote: "I acted for my country and posterity in obedience to the will of God."

James W. Grimes of Iowa, one of Johnson's bitter and influential foes in the Senate, became convinced that the trial was intended only to excite public passions through "lies sent from here by the most worthless and irresponsible creatures on the face of the earth" (an indication, perhaps, of the improved quality of Washington correspondents in the last eighty-seven years).

Unfortunately, the abuse and threats heaped upon him during the trial brought on a stroke of paralysis only two days before the vote was to be taken, and he was confined to his bed. The Radical Republicans, refusing any postponement, were delightedly certain that Grimes would either be too sick in fact to attend on May 16, or would plead that his illness prevented him from attending to cast the vote that would end his career. In the galleries, the crowd sang, "Old Grimes is dead, that bad old man, we ne'er shall see him more." And in the New York *Tribune,* Horace Greeley was writing: "It seems as if no generation could pass without giving us one man to live among the Warnings of history. We have had Benedict Arnold, Aaron Burr, Jefferson Davis, and now we have James W. Grimes."

But James W. Grimes was a man of great physical as well as moral courage, and just before the balloting was to begin on May 16, four men carried the pale and withered Senator from Iowa into his seat. He later wrote that Fessenden had grasped his hand and given him a "glorified smile. . . . I would not today exchange that recollection for the highest distinction of life." The Chief Justice suggested that it would be permissible for him to remain seated while voting—but with the assistance of his friends, Senator Grimes struggled to his feet and in a surprisingly firm voice called out, "Not guilty."

Burned in effigy, accused in the press of "idiocy and impotency," and repudiated by his state and friends, Grimes never recovered—but before he died he declared to a friend:

> I shall ever thank God that in that troubled hour of trial, when many privately confessed that they had sacrificed their judgment and their conscience at the behests of party newspapers and party hate, I had the courage to be true to my oath and my conscience. . . . Perhaps I did wrong not to commit perjury by order of a party; but I cannot see it that way. . . . I became a judge acting on my own responsibility and accountable only to my own conscience and my Maker; and no power could force me to decide on such a case contrary to my convictions, whether that party was composed of my friends or my enemies.

VII

LUCIUS QUINTUS CINCINNATUS LAMAR

"Today I Must Be True or False . . ."

No one had ever seen that hardened veteran politician, Speaker of the House James G. Blaine, cry. But there he sat, with the tears streaming unashamedly down his cheeks, unable to conceal his emotions from the full view of the House members and spectators. But few on the floor or in the galleries on that dramatic day in 1874 were paying much attention to Mr. Blaine, and most were making no attempt to hide their own tears. Democrats and Republicans alike, battle-scarred veterans of the Civil War and the violence of politics, sat in somber silence, as they listened to the urgent entreaties of the freshman Congressman from Mississippi. Speaking simply and clearly, without resorting to the customary rhetorical devices, his full, rich voice touched the hearts of every listener with its simple plea for amity and justice between North and South.

All were touched, yes, by his message; but stunned, too, by its impact—for Lucius Lamar of Mississippi was appealing in the name of the South's most implacable enemy, the Radical Republican who had helped make the

Reconstruction Period a black nightmare the South never could forget: Charles Sumner of Massachusetts. Charles Sumner—who assailed Daniel Webster as a traitor for seeking to keep the South in the Union—who helped crucify Edmund Ross for his vote against the Congressional mob rule that would have ground the South and the Presidency under its heel—whose own death was hastened by the terrible caning administered to him on the Senate floor years earlier by Congressman Brooks of South Carolina, who thereupon became a Southern hero—Charles Sumner was now dead. And Lucius Lamar, known in the prewar days as one of the most rabid "fire-eaters" ever to come out of the deep South, was standing on the floor of the House and delivering a moving eulogy lamenting his departure!

For Charles Sumner before he died, Lamar told his hushed audience,

> believed that all occasion for strife and distrust between the North and South had passed away. . . . Is not that the common sentiment—or if it is not, ought it not to be—of the great mass of our people, North and South? . . . Shall we not, over the honored remains of . . . this earnest pleader for the exercise of human tenderness and charity, lay aside the concealments which serve only to perpetuate misunderstandings and distrust, and frankly confess that on both sides we most earnestly desire to be one . . . in feeling and in heart? . . . Would that the spirit of the illustrious dead whom we lament today could speak from the grave to both parties to this deplorable discord in tones which should reach each and every heart throughout this broad territory: "My countrymen! know one another, and you will love one another!"

There was an ominous silence—a silence of both meditation and shock. Then a spontaneous burst of applause rolled out from all sides. "My God, what a speech!" said Congressman Lyman Tremaine of New York to "Pig Iron" Kelly of Pennsylvania. "It will ring through the country."

Few speeches in American political history have had such immediate impact. Overnight it raised Lamar to the first rank in the Congress and in the country; and more importantly it marked a turning point in the relations between North and South. Two weeks after the Sumner eulogy, Carl Schurz of Missouri rose before ten thousand citizens of Boston and hailed Lamar as the prophet of a new day in the relations between North and South. The Boston *Globe* called Lamar's speech on Sumner "evidence of the restoration of the Union in the South"; and the Boston *Advertiser* said it was "the most significant and hopeful utterance that has been heard from the South since the war."

It was inevitable that some, both North and South, would misunderstand it. Northerners whose political power depended on maintaining the Federal hegemony over the former Confederate states resisted any effort to heal sectional strife. James Blaine, when his tears were dry, was to write of the Sumner eulogy that "it was a mark of positive genius in a Southern representative to pronounce a fervid and discriminating eulogy upon Mr. Sumner, and skillfully interweave with it a defense of that which Mr. Sumner, like John Wesley, believed to be the sum of all villainies."

Southerners to whom Charles Sumner symbolized the worst of the prewar abolitionist movement and the postwar reconstruction felt betrayed. Several leading Mississippi newspapers, including the Columbus *Democrat,* the Canton *Mail* and the Meridian *Mercury,* vigorously criticized Lamar, as did many of his old friends, maintaining that he had surrendered Southern principle and honor. To his wife, Lamar wrote:

> No one here thinks I lowered the Southern flag, but the Southern press is down on me. . . . Our people have suffered so much, have been betrayed so often by those in whom they had the strongest reason to confide, that it is but natural that they should be suspicious of any word or act of overture to

the North by a Southern man. I know for once that I have done her good . . . that I have awakened sympathies where before existed animosities. If she condemns me, while I shall not be indifferent to her disapprobation, I shall not be . . . resentful. I shall be cheered by the thought that I have done a beneficial thing for her. It is time for a public man to try to serve the South, and not to subserve her irritated feelings. . . . I shall serve no other interest than hers, and will calmly and silently retire to private life if her people do not approve me.

Such attacks, however, were in the minority. It was generally recognized, North and South, that the speech which could have been a disaster was in fact a notable triumph. It was obvious that, moved by the strange forces of history and personal destiny, the man and the occasion had met that day in Washington.

* * *

Who was the man?

Lucius Quintus Cincinnatus Lamar was, in 1874, a "public man." No petty issues, no political trivia, not even private affairs, were permitted to clutter up his intellect. No partisan, personal or sectional considerations could outweigh his devotion to the national interest and to the truth. He was not only a statesman but also a scholar and one of the few original thinkers of his day. Henry Adams considered him to be one of "the calmest, most reasonable and most amiable men in the United States, and quite unusual in social charm. Above all . . . he had tact and humor." Henry Watterson, the famous Washington reporter, called him the "most interesting and lovable of men. . . . I rather think that Lamar was the biggest brained of all the men I have met in Washington." And Senator Hoar once remarked:

The late Matthew Arnold used to say that American public men lacked what he called "distinction." Nobody would have said that of Mr. Lamar. He would have been a conspicuous personality anywhere, with a character and quality of his own. He was a very interesting and very remarkable and very noble character.

The well-known Washington correspondent, William Preston Johnson, wrote: "The Lamars are Huguenot in origin. The fatal dowry of genius was on that house. All that came forth from it felt its touch, its inspiration, its triumph and some share of its wretchedness." A roll call in his father's home was an impressive experience; for Lucius Lamar's uncles included Mirabeau Bonaparte, whose charge at San Jacinto broke the Mexican line and made him the second President of the Texas Republic; Jefferson Jackson, Thomas Randolph, and Lavoisier LeGrand, indicating in the christener a changing interest from history to politics and from politics to chemistry. But that fatal touch of genius and melancholia had marked his father, who, at thirty-seven, with a notable career in the Georgia Bar before him, in a period of intense depression, kissed his wife and children good-by, walked into his garden and shot himself.

A similar black thread of moodiness and depression ran throughout all of Lamar's life. Although it never conquered him, his contemporaries observed his self-absorption, his sensitive and, on occasions, morose nature. His youth was on the whole, however, a happy one, on a plantation in the area where Joel Harris was to collect his Uncle Remus and Br'er Rabbit tales. Lamar himself was famous later for his stories of the rural South, as noted by Henry Adams in speaking of how effective a representative of the Confederacy Lamar would have made in London: "London society would have delighted in him; his stories would have won success; his manners would have made him loved; his oratory would have swept every audience."

Lamar from the beginning under his mother's direction showed a notable aptitude for study. Many years later he said, "Books! I was surrounded with books.

The first book I remember having had put into my hands by my mother was Franklin's *Autobiography*." The second was Rollin's *History*, the same *History* which nine-year-old John Quincy Adams had pondered over many years before. Lamar became well read in diplomacy and the law, but he was also passionately fond of light literature, as several correspondents discovered years later when they assisted Lamar in gathering several books which had accidentally spilled from his official briefcase as he entered the White House for a Cabinet meeting. They were all cheap novels!

Emory College, which Lamar attended, was a hotbed of states' rights. Its president, a member of the celebrated Longstreet family, was a flaming follower of Calhoun, and his influence over Lamar, always strong, increased when Lamar married his daughter. When Longstreet left Georgia to take over the presidency of the State University at Oxford, Mississippi, Lamar accompanied him to practice law and to teach, and it was while at the university that Lamar was presented with the opportunity which commenced his public career.

On March 5, 1850, the Legislature of the State of Mississippi adopted a series of resolutions instructing the representatives of Mississippi to vote against the admission of California. When Senator Foote disregarded these instructions in a noticeable display of courage, Lamar was prevailed upon by a committee of states' rights Democrats to debate the Senator upon the latter's return to Mississippi to run for Governor. Lamar was only twenty-six years of age, new to the state and the political life of his day, and was given only a few hours to prepare for debate against one of the most skilled and aggressive politicians of the times. But his extemporaneous speech, in which he chastised Senator Foote for ignoring the instructions of the Mississippi Legislature, (as he himself was to do twenty-eight years later) was a notable success, and at the end of the debate the students of the university "bore him away upon their shoulders."

His election to Congress as a strong supporter of the doctrines of Calhoun and Jefferson Davis followed. In Congress, while Alexander Stephens, Robert Toombs, and other Southern Unionists were vainly seeking to stem the sectional tide, Lamar was violently pro-Southern. "Others may boast," he said on the floor of the House, "of their widely extended patriotism, and their enlarged and comprehensive love of this Union. With me, I confess that the promotion of Southern interests is second in importance only to the preservation of Southern honor." Some years later he said that he never entertained a doubt of the soundness of the Southern system until he found out that slavery could not stand a war. He did not proceed, however, on his course unmindful of its certain end. In a letter he wrote: "Dissolution cannot take place quietly. . . . When the sun of the Union sets it will go down in blood."

By 1860 he passed, in the words of Henry Adams, "for the worst of the Southern fire-eaters." Having lost all hope that the South could obtain justice in the Federal Union, he walked out of the Democratic Convention in Charleston with Jefferson Davis, helping to break still another link in the chain of Union. His prewar career reached its climax in 1861 when he drafted the ordinance of secession dissolving Mississippi's ties with the Union. The wind had been sown; now Lamar and Mississippi were to reap the whirlwind.

On both it fell with equal violence. Certainly many of the trials and much of the agony which dogged the South in the years after the war were due to the loss in the struggle of those who might have been expected to assert the leadership of the region. Control in government had always been narrowly held in the South, compared to the North, and among the ruling families "the spilling of the wine" was especially heavy. Of the thirteen descendants of the first Lamar in America who served in the Confederate Armies with the rank of lieutenant colonel or above, seven perished in the war. Lamar's youngest brother, supposedly the most brilliant, Jefferson Mirabeau, was killed as he leaped his horse over the enemy's breastworks at Crampton's Gap. His cousin John, one of the largest slaveholders in the South, fell near him. Two years later Lamar's older brother, Thompson Bird, Colonel of the Fifth Florida, was killed in the bloody fighting at Petersburg. Lamar's two law partners were both killed: Colonel Mott at Williamsburg where Lamar fought at his side, and James Autrey, in the slaughter at Murfreesboro. Symbolic of the dark days that were coming, the shattered office shingle bearing the names of the three partners was found floating in the river.

Lamar's own military career was ended by an attack of apoplexy, a disease from which he suffered throughout his entire life and which hung over him like death in moments of high excitement. He served nearly all of the remainder of the war as a diplomatic agent for the Confederate Government.

With the end of the war which had blasted all of Lamar's hopes and illusions, he was under strong pressure to leave the wreck of the past and go to another country. He felt, in the words of his biographer, Wirt Armistead Cate, that he was discredited—a leader who had carried his people into the wilderness from which there had been no return. But he followed Robert Lee's advice to the leaders of the South to remain and "share the fate of their respective states," and from 1865 to 1872 Lamar lived quietly in Mississippi teaching and practicing law, as his state passed through the bitter days of its reconstruction.

No state suffered more from carpetbag rule than Mississippi. Adelbert Ames, first Senator and then Governor, was a native of Maine, a son-in-law of the notorious "butcher of New Orleans," Ben Butler. He admitted before a Congressional committee that only his election to the Senate prompted him to take up his residence in Mississippi. He was chosen Governor by a majority composed of freed slaves and Radical Republicans, sustained and nourished by Federal bayonets. One Cardoza, under indictment for larceny in New York, was placed at the head of the public schools and two former slaves held the offices of Lieutenant Governor and Secretary of State. Vast areas of northern Mississippi lay in ruins. Taxes increased to a level fourteen times as high as normal in order to support the extravagances of the reconstruction government and heavy state and national war debts.

As he passed through these troubled times, Lamar came to understand that the sole hope for the South lay not in pursuing its ancient quarrels with the North but in promoting conciliation and in the development and restitution of normal Federal-state relations and the withdrawal of military rule. This in turn could only be accomplished by making the North comprehend that the South no longer desired—in Lamar's words—to be the "agitator and agitated pendulum of American politics." Lamar hoped to make the North realize that the abrogation of the Constitutional guarantees of the people of the South must inevitably affect the liberties of the people of the North. He came to believe that the future happiness of the country could only lie in a spirit of mutual conciliation and cooperation between the people of all sections and all states.

There were two forces in opposition to his policy. On the one hand were those Republican leaders who believed that only by waving the bloody shirt could they maintain their support in the North and East, particularly among the Grand Army of the Republic; and who were convinced by the elections of 1868 that, if the Southern states should once again be controlled by the Democrats, those states—together with their allies in the

North—would make the Republicans a permanent minority nationally. On the other hand there were those in the South who traveled the easy road to influence and popularity through pandering to and exploiting the natural resentment and bitterness of the defeated South against its occupiers.

In contrast, Lamar believed that "the only course I, in common with other Southern representatives have to follow, is to do what we can to allay excitement between the sections and to bring about peace and reconciliation."

In 1872 he was elected to Congress, and his petition for a pardon from the disabilities imposed on all Confederate officials by the Fourteenth Amendment was granted. Sumner's death, and the invitation of Representative Hoar of Massachusetts to pronounce the eulogy, furnished the ideal occasion for which Lamar had long waited to hold out the hand of friendship to the North. Everything conspired to insure his success: his prewar reputation as a disunionist, his service as a Confederate official, the fact that Sumner was widely hated in Mississippi and in the South, and his own exceptional skill as an orator. All these factors in his favor were reinforced by his impressive personal appearance—including, in the words of Henry Grady, "that peculiar swarthy complexion, pale but clear; the splendid gray eyes, the high cheekbones; dark brown hair, the firm fixed mouth." His memorable eulogy of Sumner was Lucius Lamar's first opportunity to demonstrate a new kind of Southern statesmanship. But it would not be his last.

* * *

Mississippians, on the whole, came either to understand and admire the sentiments of the Sumner eulogy, to respect Lamar's sincerity if they did not admire it, or to forgive him for what they considered to be one serious error of judgment if they were strongly opposed to it. Riding a wave of popularity and the 1876 return to Democratic rule in Mississippi, Lamar was elected by the Legislature to the United States Senate. But even before he moved from the House to the Senate, Lamar again outraged many of his backers by abandoning his party and section on another heated issue.

The Hayes-Tilden Presidential contest of 1876 had been a bitter struggle, apparently culminating in a close electoral-vote victory for the Democrat Tilden. Although Hayes at first accepted his defeat with philosophic resignation, his lieutenants, with the cooperation of the Republican *New York Times*, converted the apparent certainty of Tilden's election into doubt by claiming the closely contested states of South Carolina, Louisiana and Florida—and then attempted to convert that doubt into the certainty of Hayes' election by procuring from the carpetbag governments of those three states doctored election returns. With rumors of violence and military dictatorship rife, Congress determined upon arbitration by a supposedly nonpartisan Electoral Commission—and Lucius Lamar, confident that an objective inquiry would demonstrate the palpable fraud of the Republican case, agreed to this solution to prevent a recurrence of the tragic conflict which had so aged his spirit and broadened his outlook.

But when the Commission, acting wholly along party lines, awarded the disputed states and the election to Hayes with 185 electoral votes to 184 for Tilden, the South was outraged. Four more years of Republican rule meant four more years of Southern bondage and exploitation, four more years before the South could regain her dignity and her rightful place in the nation. Lamar was accused of trading his vote and his section's honor for a promise of a future position; he was accused of cowardice, of being afraid to stand up for his state when it meant a fight; and he was accused of deserting his people and his party in the very hour when triumph should have been at last rightfully theirs. His enemies, realizing that six years would pass before Senator-elect Lamar would be forced to run for re-election, vowed never to forget that day of perfidy.

But Lucius Lamar, a man of law and honor, could not now repudiate the findings, however shocking, of the Commission he had helped establish. He supported the findings of the Commission because he believed that only force could prevent Hayes' inaugural and that it would be disastrous to travel that road again. It was better, he believed, for the South—in spite of provocation—to accept defeat on this occasion. He was skillful enough, however, to get Hayes committed to concessions for the South, including the withdrawal of military occupation forces and a return to Home Rule in key states. This genuine service to his state, on an occasion when many Southern politicians were talking of open defiance, was at first largely obscured. But unmoved by the storm of opposition which poured forth from Mississippi, Lamar braced himself in preparation for the most crucial test of his role as a nonsectional, nonpartisan statesman which lay ahead in the Senate.

No other high-ranking Confederate officer had yet entered the Senate. Nor had many Senators forgotten that nearly twenty years earlier Lamar was an extreme sectionalist Congressman, who had resigned his seat to draft the Mississippi Ordinance of Secession. The time was not auspicious for his return. The Republicans were already accusing the Democrats of harboring insurrectionists and traitors; and the Democratic contribution to increased intersectional distrust was a new breed of Southern demagogues, intolerant and vengeful, "sired by Reconstruction out of scalawags."

As Senator Lamar, ill and fatigued, rested at home throughout much of 1877, a new movement was sweeping the South and West, a movement which would plague the political parties of the nation for a generation to come—"free silver." The Moses of the silver forces, William Jennings Bryan, had not yet appeared on the scene; but "Silver Dick" Bland, the Democratic Representative from Missouri, was leading the way with his bill for the free coinage of all silver brought to the Mint. Inasmuch as a tremendous spurt in the production of the Western silver mines had caused its value in relation to gold to shrink considerably, the single purpose of the silver forces was clear, simple and appealing—easy, inflationary money.

It was a tremendously popular cause in Mississippi. The panic of 1873 had engulfed the nation into the most terrible depression it had ever suffered, and the already impoverished states of the South were particularly hard hit. Businesses failed by the thousands, unemployment increased and wages were reduced. Farm prices dropped rapidly from their high wartime levels and the farmers of Mississippi—desperate for cash—vowed support of any bill which would raise the price of their commodities, lower the value of the debts, and increase the availability of money. The South foresaw itself in a state of permanent indebtedness to the financial institutions of the East unless easy money could be made available to pay its heavy debts.

Vachel Lindsay's poem expressed clearly the helplessness and bitterness with which the South and West watched the steadily increasing financial domination of the East:

> And all these in their helpless days
> By the dour East oppressed,
> Mean paternalism
> Making their mistakes for them,
> Crucifying half the West,
> Till the whole Atlantic coast
> Seemed a giant spiders' nest.

Silver suddenly acquired a political appeal as the poor man's friend—in contrast to gold, the rich man's money; silver was the money of the prairies and small towns, unlike gold, the money of Wall Street. Silver was going to provide an easy solution to everyone's problems—falling farm prices, high interest rates, heavy debts and all the rest. Although the Democratic party since the days of Jackson and Benton had been the party of hard money, it rushed to exploit this new and popular issue—and it was naturally assumed that the freshman Democratic Senator from poverty-stricken Mississippi would enthusiastically join the fight.

But Lamar, the learned scholar and professor, approached the issue somewhat differently than his colleagues. Paying but little heed to the demands of his constituents, he exhausted all available treatises on both sides of the controversy. His study convinced him—possibly wrongly—that the only sound position was in support of sound money. The payment of our government's debts—even to the "bloated bondholders" of Wall Street—in a debased, inflated currency, as the Bland Bill encouraged and the accompanying Matthews Resolution specifically provided, was an ethical wrong and a practical mistake, he felt, certain to embarrass our standing in the eyes of the world, and promoted not as a permanent financial program but as a spurious relief bill to alleviate the nation's economic distress.

On January 24, 1878, in a courageous and learned address—his first major speech on the Senate floor—Lamar rejected the pleas of Mississippi voters and assailed elaborate rationalizations behind the two silver measures as artificial and exaggerated. And the following day he voted "No" on the Matthews Resolution, in opposition to his colleague from Mississippi, a Negro Republican of exceptional talents elected several years earlier by the old "carpetbag" Legislature.

Praise for Senator Lamar's masterly and statesmanlike analysis of the issue emanated from many parts of the country, but from Mississippi came little but condemnation. On January 30, the State Legislature adopted a Memorial omitting all mention of Lamar but—in an obvious and deliberate slap—congratulating and thanking his colleague (to whom the white Democratic legislators normally were bitterly opposed) for voting the opposite way and thus reflecting "the sentiment and will of his constituents." The Memorial deeply hurt Lamar, and he was little consoled by a letter from his close friend, the Speaker of the Mississippi House, who termed it "a damned outrage" but explained:

> The people are under a pressure of hard times and scarcity of money, and their representatives felt bound to strike at something which might give relief, the how or wherefor very few of them could explain.

But the Legislature was not through. On February 4, a resolution was passed by both Houses instructing Lamar to vote for the Bland Silver Bill, and to use his efforts as spokesman for Mississippi to secure its passage.

Lamar was deeply troubled by this action. He knew that the right of binding legislative instructions had firm roots in the South. But writing to his wife about the demands of the Legislature that had appointed him, he confided, "I cannot do it; I had rather quit politics forever." He attempted to explain at length to a friend in the Legislature that he recognized the right of that body to express its opinions upon questions of federal policy, and the obligation of a Senator to abide by those expressions whenever he was doubtful as to what his course should be. But in this particular case, he insisted, "their wishes are directly in conflict with the convictions of my whole life; and had I voted [on the Matthews Resolution] as directed, I should have cast my first vote against my conscience."

> If [a Senator] allows himself to be governed by the opinions of his friends at home, however devoted he may be to them or they to him, he throws away all the rich results of a previous preparation and study, and simply becomes a commonplace exponent of those popular sentiments which may change in a few days. . . . Such a course will dwarf any man's statesmanship and his vote would be simply considered as an echo of current opinion, not the result of mature deliberations.

Moreover, consistent with the courageous philosophy that had governed his return to public life, Lamar was determined not to back down merely because his section was contrary minded. He would not purchase the respect of the North for himself and his section by a calculated and cringing course; but having decided, on the merits, that the bill was wrong, he was anxious to demonstrate to the nation that statesmanship was not dead in the South nor was the South desirous of repudiating national obligations and honor. He felt that on this issue it was of particular importance that the South should not follow a narrow sectional course of action. For years it had been argued that Southern Democrats would seek to abrogate the obligations that the United States Government had incurred during the Civil War and for which the South felt no responsibility. Lamar alone among the Southern Democrats opposed the "free silver" movement, except for Senator Ben Hill of Georgia, who said that while he had done his best during the war to make the Union bondholder who purchased a dollar bond at sixty cents lose the sixty cents he had given, he was now for repaying him the dollar he was promised.

One week later, the Bland Silver Bill came before the Senate for a final vote. As the debate neared its end, Senator Lamar rose unexpectedly to his feet. No notes were in his hand, for he was one of the most brilliant extemporaneous speakers ever to sit in the Senate. ("The pen is an extinguisher upon my mind," he said, "and a torture to my nerves.") Instead he held an official document which bore the great seal of the State of Mississippi, and this he dispatched by page to the desk. With apologies to his colleagues, Senator Lamar explained that, although he had already expressed his views on the Silver Bill, he had "one other duty to perform; a very painful one, but one which is nonetheless clear." He then asked that the resolutions which he had sent to the desk be read.

The Senate was first astonished and then attentively silent as the Clerk droned the express will of the Mississippi Legislature that its Senators vote for the Bland Silver Bill. As the Clerk completed the instructions, all eyes turned toward Lamar, no one certain what to expect. As the reporter for the Washington *Capitol* described it:

> Remembering the embarrassing position of this gentleman with respect to the pending bill, every Senator immediately gave his attention, and the Chamber became as silent as the tomb.

A massive but lonely figure on the Senate floor, Lucius Lamar spoke in a quiet yet powerful voice, a voice which "grew tremulous with emotion, as his body fairly shook with agitation":

> Mr. President: Between these resolutions and my convictions there is a great gulf. I cannot pass it. . . . Upon the youth of my state whom it has been my privilege to assist in education I have always endeavored to impress the belief that truth was better than falsehood, honesty better than policy, courage better than cowardice. Today my lessons confront me. Today I must be true or false, honest or cunning, faithful or unfaithful to my people. Even in this hour of their legislative displeasure and disapprobation, I cannot vote as these resolutions direct.
>
> My reasons for my vote shall be given to my people. Then it will be for them to determine if adherence to my honest convictions has disqualified me from representing them;

whether a difference of opinion upon a difficult and complicated subject to which I have given patient, long-continued, conscientious study, to which I have brought entire honesty and singleness of purpose, and upon which I have spent whatever ability God has given me, is now to separate us; . . . but be their present decision what it may, I know that the time is not far distant when they will recognize my action today as wise and just; and, armed with honest convictions of my duty, I shall calmly await the results, believing in the utterance of a great American that "truth is omnipotent, and public justice certain."

Senators on both sides of the bill immediately crowded about his desk to commend his courage. Lamar knew that his speech and vote could not prevent passage of the Bland Bill by a tremendous margin, and its subsequent enactment over the veto of President Hayes. Yet his intentional and stunningly courageous disobedience to the will of his constituents was not wholly in vain. Throughout the North the speech was highly praised. Distrust toward the South, and suspicion of its attitude toward the national debt and national credit, diminished. *Harper's Weekly,* pointing out that Lamar voted in opposition to "the strong and general public feeling of his state" concluded:

No Senator has shown himself more worthy of universal respect than Mr. Lamar; for none has stood more manfully by his principles, in the face of the most authoritative remonstrance from his state. . . . The Democratic Senator from Mississippi has shown the manly courage which becomes an American statesman.

The Nation editorialized that the brief speech of Lucius Lamar in explanation of his disregard for the instructions of his state, "for manliness, dignity and pathos has never been surpassed in Congress. His vote will probably cost him his seat."

This prediction seemed certain of fulfillment. The assault upon the Senator in Mississippi was instantaneous and vigorous. He had turned his back on his people and his section. In the words of one political orator, he had "made such haste to join the ranks of the enemy that he went stumbling over the graves of his fallen comrades." His old friend Jefferson Davis hurt him deeply by publicly condemning Lamar's disregard of the Legislature's instructions as an attack upon "the foundation of our political system" and the long-standing practice of the Southern Democratic party. To refuse either to obey or to resign the office, so that his constituents "might select someone else who might truly represent them," was to deny, said Davis, that the people had the requisite amount of intelligence to govern! (Lamar was hard hit by the attitude of his former chieftain, but it is illuminating to note that a few days later, when Senator Hoar sought to deny Davis the Mexican War Pension to which he was by law entitled, it was Lamar who spoke for the Confederate leader in a memorable and dramatic defense:

> Sir, it required no courage to do that; . . . the gentleman, I believe, takes rank among the Christian statesmen. He might have learned a better lesson from the pages of mythology. When Prometheus was bound to the rock, it was not an eagle, it was a vulture that buried his beak in the tortured vitals of the victim.

According to a contemporary account, as Lamar hissed out, "it was a vulture," his right arm straightened out and the index finger pointed directly at Hoar.)

All agreed that Lamar was politically dead after one term, and the only question was who would succeed him. Lamar loved Mississippi, and its criticism depressed him deeply. He wrote his wife that he wished he was in a financial position to vacate his office without doing his family injustice:

> This world is a miserable one to me except in its connection with you. . . . I get a great many complimentary

letters from the North, very few from Mississippi. . . . Can it be true that the South will condemn the disinterested love of those who, perceiving her real interests, offer their unarmored breasts as barriers against the invasion of error? . . . It is indeed a heavy cross to lay upon the heart of a public man to have to take a stand which causes the love and confidence of his constituents to flow away from him.

But like his famous uncle, Mirabeau Lamar of Texas, and other members of his family, Lucius Quintus Cincinnatus Lamar was not afraid of overwhelming odds. Admittedly he had violated the instructions of the Legislature, he said. "I will appeal to the sovereign people, the masters of the legislature who undertake to instruct me."

With this declaration, Senator Lamar launched successive tours of Mississippi. Speaking to thousands of people in crowded halls and open fields, Lamar stated frankly that he was well aware that he had not pleased his constituents; that he was equally well aware that the easier path was to exploit that sectional cause to which he had always been devoted; but that it was his intention to help create a feeling of confidence and mutuality between North and South by voting in the national interest without regard to sectional pressures.

For three or four hours at a time, his passionate and imaginative oratory held spellbound the crowds that came to jeer. "He spoke like the mountain torrent," as several observers later described it, "sweeping away the boulders in the stream that attempted to oppose his course."

But Lamar did not employ oratorical tricks to sway emotions while dodging issues. On the contrary, his speeches were a learned explanation of his position, setting forth the Constitutional history of the Senate and its relationship to the state legislatures, and the statements and examples of Burke, and of Calhoun, Webster, and other famous Senators who had disagreed with

Legislative instructions: "Better to follow the example of the illustrious men whose names have been given than to abandon altogether judgment and conviction in deference to popular clamor."

At each meeting he told of an incident which he swore had occurred during the war. Lamar, in the company of other prominent military and civilian officers of the Confederacy, was on board a blockade runner making for Savannah harbor. Although the high-ranking officers after consultation had decided it was safe to go ahead, Lamar related, the Captain had sent Sailor Billy Summers to the top mast to look for Yankee gunboats in the harbor, and Billy said he had seen ten. That distinguished array of officers knew where the Yankee fleet was, and it was *not* in Savannah; and they told the Captain that Billy was wrong and the ship must proceed ahead. The Captain refused, insisting that while the officers knew a great deal more about military affairs, Billy Summers on the top mast with a powerful glass had a much better opportunity to judge the immediate situation at hand.

It later developed that Billy was right, Lamar said, and if they had gone ahead they would have all been captured. And like Sailor Billy Summers, he did not claim to be wiser than the Mississippi Legislature. But he did believe that he was in a better position as a Member of the United States Senate to judge what was best for the interests of his constituents.

Thus it is, my countrymen, you have sent me to the topmost mast, and I tell you what I see. If you say I must come down, I will obey without a murmur, for you cannot make me lie to you; but if you return me, I can only say that I will be true to love of country, truth, and God. . . . I have always thought that the first duty of a public man in a Republic founded upon the sovereignty of the people is a frank and sincere expression of his opinions to his constituents. I prize the confidence of the people of Mississippi, but

I never made popularity the standard of my action. I profoundly respect public opinion, but I believe that there is in conscious rectitude of purpose a sustaining power which will support a man of ordinary firmness under any circumstances whatever.

His tour was tremendously successful. "Men who were so hostile that they could hardly be persuaded to hear him at all would mount upon the benches and tables, swinging their hats, and huzzaing until hoarse." Others departed in silence, weighing the significance of his words. When he spoke in Yazoo County, the stronghold of his opposition, the Yazoo City *Herald* reported that like "the lion at bay," he "conquered the prejudices of hundreds who had been led to believe that his views on certain points were better adapted to the latitude of New England than to that of Mississippi." And shortly thereafter, the Yazoo Democratic County Convention adopted a resolution that their legislators should "vote for him and work for him, first, last, and all the time, as the choice of this people for United States Senator."

It is heartening to note that the people of Mississippi continued their support of him, in spite of the fact that on three important occasions—in his eulogy of Charles Sumner, in his support of the Electoral commission which brought about the election of the Republican Hayes and in his exception to their strongly felt stand for free silver—Lamar had stood against their immediate wishes. The voters responded to the sincerity and courage which he had shown; and they continued to give him their support and affection throughout the remainder of his political life. He was re-elected to the Senate by an overwhelming majority, later to become Chairman of the Senate Democratic Caucus, then Secretary of the Interior and finally Justice of the Supreme Court of the United States. At no time did he, who has properly been termed the most gifted statesman given by the South to the nation from the close of the Civil War to the turn of the century, ever veer from the deep conviction he had expressed while under bitter attack in 1878:

> The liberty of this country and its great interests will never be secure if its public men become mere menials to do the biddings of their constituents instead of being representatives in the true sense of the word, looking to the lasting prosperity and future interests of the whole country.

PART FOUR

The Time and the Place

Two men of integrity—both Republicans, both Midwesterners, but wholly dissimilar in their political philosophies and personal mannerisms—best illustrate the impact of the twentieth century upon the Senate as a whole and the atmosphere of political courage in particular. George W. Norris and Robert A. Taft, whose careers in the Senate overlapped for only a brief period some seventeen years ago, were masters of the legislative process, leaders of fundamentally opposed political factions, and expounders, each in his own way, of great constitutional doctrines. And not among the least of their accomplishments was the increased prestige and respect which they and others like them brought to the United States Senate. For, at the turn of the century, the route to fame and power for men of ability and talent had been in industry, not in politics. And as a result, the attitude of the public toward the political profession had too often been characterized by apathy, indifference, disrespect and even amusement.

The Senate had shared in the political profession's loss of prestige. It was due in part to the public reaction to the new type of legislator who too often, in 1900, included the swollen corporation lawyer and the squalid political boss. The Senate seemed to have little of the excitement and drama that had been so much a part of its existence in the years leading up to the Civil War, little of the power and prestige which it wielded so brazenly in the days of the Johnson and Grant administrations. It was in part a reaction to the increasing complexity and multiplicity of legislative issues—even Santo Domingo seemed much farther away than Fort Sumter (for blocking his Santo Domingo treaty, the Senate was told by Teddy Roosevelt that it was "wholly incompetent"), and "interstate commerce" seemed much less exciting and promising than "free silver." No longer were the names of famous Senators familiar household words, as in the days of the great triumvirate. No longer did the entire nation breathlessly follow Senate debates, as in the days of the Great Compromise or the Johnson impeachment. The nation's brightest schoolboys, who sixty or seventy years earlier would have memorized Webster's reply to Hayne, were no longer interested in politics as a career.

Those citizens who did take an active interest in the conduct of the Senate as the twentieth century got under way generally viewed it more with alarm than with pride. Throughout the nation there arose a remarkable array of reformers, muckrakers and good-government movements, represented in the Senate by a new breed of idealists and independents, men of ability and statesmanship who would have ranked with the more famous names of an earlier day. To arrest the dual trends of an electorate indifferent to their Senators and Senators indifferent to their electorate, the reformers, both in and out of the Senate, finally accomplished a long overdue change in the election machinery—the power of electing Senators was taken from the legislatures of the states and given directly to the people.

The Seventeenth Amendment, ratified in 1913, reflected a far different attitude toward the "masses" of voters than the distrust with which they were regarded in 1787 by the creators of the Constitution—but it also reflected a general decline in the respect for state legislatures, which had too often permitted powerful lobbyists and political machines to usurp their sacred right of selecting Senators. A railroad president told William Lyon Phelps that he had never desired to be a United States Senator himself, because he had made so many of them. Referring to this, a prominent New England Senator, W. E. Chandler, laconically explained his retirement to private life by saying that he had been "run over by a railroad train."

That the Seventeenth Amendment almost immediately made the Senate more responsive to popular will, both in theory and in fact, cannot be doubted; but its effects were not as far reaching nor was the complexion and make-up of the Senate changed as greatly as the reformers had hoped. Senator Boies Penrose, the boss of Pennsylvania, said to a reformer friend:

> Give me the People, every time! Look at me! No legislature would ever have dared to elect me to the Senate, not even at Harrisburg. But the People, the dear People elected me by a bigger majority than my opponent's total vote by over half a million. You and your "reformer" friends thought direct election would turn men like me out of the Senate! Give me the People, every time!

There was (and is) no way of measuring statistically or scientifically the effect of the direct election of Senators on the quality of the Senate itself. There has been no scarcity of either contemptuous criticism or lavish praise for both the Senate as a whole and individual Senators. But too often such judgments consist of generalizations from limited cases or experiences. Woodrow Wilson, for example, shortly before his death, buffeted by the Senate in his efforts on behalf of the League of Nations and the Versailles Treaty, rejected the suggestion that he seek a seat in the Senate from New Jersey, stating: "Outside of the United States, the Senate does not amount to a damn. And inside the United States the Senate is mostly despised; they haven't had a thought down there in fifty years." There are many who agreed with Wilson in 1920, and some who might agree with those sentiments today.

But Professor Woodrow Wilson, prior to his baptism of political fire, had regarded the Senate as one of the ablest and most powerful legislative bodies in the world. In part this power, and the ability it required in those Senators who sought to harness it, sprang from the growing influence of Federal legislation in domestic affairs. But even more important was the Senate's gradually increasing power in the field of foreign affairs—a power which multiplied as our nation's stature in the community of nations grew, a power which made the Senate in the twentieth century a far more significant body, in terms of the actual consequences of its decisions, than the glittering Senate of Webster, Clay and Calhoun, which had toiled endlessly but fruitlessly over the slavery question.

And just as a nation torn by internal crisis had demanded Senators of courage in 1850, so did a nation plunged into international crisis. John Quincy Adams had realized this one hundred years before George Norris ever came to Washington. But he could not have foreseen that this nation's role in the world would bring constantly recurring crises and troublesome problems to the floor of the United States Senate, crises which would force men like George Norris to choose between conscience and constituents, problems which would force men like Bob Taft to choose between principles and popularity.

These are not the only stories of political courage in

the twentieth century, possibly not even the most outstanding or significant. Yet the changing nature of the Senate, its work and its members, seems to have lessened the frequency with which the nation is given inspiration by a selfless stand for great but unpopular principles. Perhaps we are still too close in time to those in our own midst whose actions a more detached historical perspective may someday stamp as worthy of recording in the annals of political courage. Perhaps the twentieth-century Senator is not called upon to risk his entire future on one basic issue in the manner of Edmund Ross or Thomas Hart Benton. Perhaps our modern acts of political courage do not arouse the public in the manner that crushed the career of Sam Houston and John Quincy Adams. Still, when we realize that a newspaper that chooses to denounce a Senator today can reach many thousand times as many voters as could be reached by all of Daniel Webster's famous and articulate detractors put together, these stories of twentieth-century political courage have a drama, an excitement—and an inspiration—all their own.

VIII

GEORGE NORRIS

"I HAVE COME HOME TO TELL YOU THE TRUTH."

At precisely 1:00 P.M. one wintry afternoon early in 1910, Representative John Dalzell of Pennsylvania left the Speaker's Chair and walked out of the House Chamber for his daily cup of coffee and piece of pie in the Capitol restaurant. His departure was not unusual—for Representative Dalzell, who was Speaker Joe Cannon's first assistant in ruling the House from the Speaker's Chair, had always left the Chamber at exactly that hour, and he was almost invariably succeeded in the Chair by Representative Walter Smith of Iowa. But on that particular January afternoon Representative Dalzell's journey up the aisle was watched with curious satisfaction by a somewhat shaggy-looking Representative in a plain black suit and a little shoe-string tie. And the Assistant Speaker had no sooner reached the door of the Chamber when Republican Representative George W. Norris of Nebraska walked over to Representative Smith and asked if he might be recognized for two minutes. Smith, a member of the Cannon-Dalzell Republican ruling clique but a personal friend of Norris', agreed.

To his astonishment, Representative Norris sought to amend the resolution then under debate—a resolution calling for a joint committee to investigate the Ballinger-Pinchot conservation dispute—by requiring the entire House of Representatives to appoint its members to the investigating committee, instead of granting the customary authority to the Speaker to make such selections.

Page boys scurried out to find Cannon and Dalzell. This was insurrection in the ranks—the first attempt to limit the previously unlimited power of "Czar" Cannon! But Norris insisted that all he desired was a fair investigation, not one rigged by the administration. Joined by Pinchot followers, fellow insurgent Republicans and practically all of the Democrats, he succeeded in having his amendment adopted by the narrow margin of 149 to 146.

It was the first setback the powerful Speaker had ever suffered, and he vowed never to forget it. But for George Norris, the victory on the investigation resolution was only a preliminary step. For in the inner pocket of his threadbare black coat was a scrawled resolution which he had drafted years before—a resolution to have the House, rather than the Speaker, appoint the members of the Rules Committee itself, the Committee which completely dictated the House program and was in turn completely dominated by the Speaker.

On St. Patrick's Day in 1910, Norris rose to address the "Czar." Only minutes before, Cannon had ruled that a census bill promoted by one of his cohorts was privileged under the Constitution and could be considered out of order, inasmuch as that document provided for the taking of the census. "Mr. Speaker," called Norris, "I present a resolution made privileged by the Constitution." "The gentleman will present it," replied Cannon, smugly unaware of the attack about to be launched. And George Norris unfolded that tattered paper from his coat pocket and asked the Clerk to read it aloud.

Panic broke out in the Republican leadership. Cloakroom rumors had previously indicated the nature of Norris' proposed resolution—but it was merely a subject of contemptuous amusement among the regular Republicans, who knew they had the power to bury it forever in the Rules Committee itself. Now Cannon's own ruling on the census bill in support of his friend had given Norris—and his resolution, clearly based on the Constitution's provision for House rules—an opening, an opening through which the Nebraska Congressman led all of the insurgent and Democratic forces. Cannon and his lieutenants were masters of parliamentary maneuvering and they were not immediately ready to coincide. They attempted to adjourn, to recess, to make a quorum impossible. They continued debate on whether the resolution was privileged while the party faithful hurried back from St. Patrick's Day parades. They kept the House in constant session, hoping to break the less organized revolters. All night long the insurgents stayed in their seats, unwilling to nap off the floor for fear that Cannon would suddenly rule in their absence.

Finally, all attempts at intimidation and compromise having failed, Speaker Cannon, as expected, ruled the resolution out of order; and Norris promptly appealed the decision. By a vote of 182 to 160, Democrats and insurgent Republicans overruled the Speaker, and by a still larger margin Norris' resolution—already amended to obtain Democratic support—was adopted. The most ruthless and autocratic Speaker in the history of the House of Representatives thereupon submitted his resignation; but George Norris, who insisted his fight was to end the dictatorial power of the office rather than to punish the individual, voted against its acceptance. Years later, Cannon was to say to him:

Norris, throughout our bitter controversy, I do not recall a single instance in which you have been unfair. I cannot say this of many of your associates; and I want to say to you now that if any member of your damned gang had to be elected to the Senate, I would prefer it be you more than any of them.

The overthrow of Cannonism broke the strangle hold which the conservative Republican leaders had held over the Government and the nation; and it also ended whatever favors the Representative from Nebraska had previously received at their hands. Under the "Czar," the office of the Speaker of the House wielded what sometimes appeared to be very nearly equal power with the President and the entire United States Senate. It was a power that placed party above all other considerations, a power that fed on party loyalty, patronage and political organizations. It was a power which, despite increasing disfavor in all parts of the country outside the East, had continued unchallenged for years. But "one man without position," an editor commented, "against 200 welded into the most powerful political machine that Washington has ever known, has twice beaten them at their own game. Mr. George Norris is a man worth knowing and watching."

* * *

George W. Norris *was* worth watching, for his subsequent career in the Senate, to which he was elected shortly after his triumph over Cannon, earned him a reputation as one of the most courageous figures in American political life. The overthrow of Cannonism, although welcomed in Nebraska by all but a few party stalwarts, had nevertheless required tremendous courage and leadership on the part of a young Congressman attacking his party's well-entrenched leaders and willing to sacrifice the comforts and alliances that party loyalty brings. In the Senate he frequently broke not only with his party but with his constituents as well. He once declared:

I would rather go down to my political grave with a clear conscience than ride in the chariot of victory as a Congressional stool pigeon, the slave, the servant, or the vassal of any man, whether he be the owner and manager of a legislative menagerie or the ruler of a great nation. . . . I would rather lie in the silent grave, remembered by both friends and enemies as one who remained true to his faith and who never faltered in what he believed to be his duty, than to still live, old and aged, lacking the confidence of both factions.

These are the words of an idealist, an independent, a fighter—a man of deep conviction, fearless courage, sincere honesty—George W. Norris of Nebraska. We should not pretend that he was a faultless paragon of virtue; on the contrary, he was, on more than one occasion, emotional in his deliberations, vituperative in his denunciations, and prone to engage in bitter and exaggerated personal attack instead of concentrating his fire upon the merits of an issue. But nothing could sway him from what he thought was right, from his determination to help all the people, from his hope to save them from the twin tragedies of poverty and war.

George Norris knew well the tragedy of poverty from his own boyhood. His father having died when George was only four, he was obliged while still in his teens to hack out a livelihood for his mother and ten sisters on the stump-covered farm lands of Ohio. He knew, too, the horrors of war, from the untimely death in the Civil War of the older brother he hardly remembered, but whose inspiring letter—written by the wounded soldier shortly before his death—was treasured by young George for years. In 1917, as the nation teetered on the edge of the European conflict, George Norris had not forgotten his mother's sorrow and her hatred of war.

A country teacher, a small-town lawyer, a local prosecuting attorney and judge—those had been the years when George Norris had come to know the people of

Nebraska and the West, when he saw the growing pattern of farm foreclosures, lost homesteads and farm workers drifting to the city and to unemployment.

As the old nineteenth century became the new twentieth, America was changing, her industries and cities were growing, her power in the world was increasing. And yet George Norris changed—and would change—very little. His chunky figure was still clothed in the drab black suits, white shirts and little black shoestring ties he had worn most of his life and would wear until his death. His mild manners, disarming honesty and avoidance of the social circle of politics in favor of a quiet evening of reading set him apart from the career politicians of his country, whose popularity among the voters, however, he far outstripped.

Only his political outlook changed as he began the long career which would keep him in Washington for forty years. For when George Norris had first entered the House of Representatives in 1903, fresh from the plains of Nebraska, he had been a staunch, conservative Republican, "sure of my position," as he later wrote, "unreasonable in my convictions, and unbending in my opposition to any other political party or political thought except my own." But "one by one I saw my favorite heroes wither . . . I discovered that my party . . . was guilty of virtually all the evils that I had charged against the opposition."

No single chapter could recount in full all of the courageous and independent battles led by George Norris. His most enduring accomplishments were in the field of public power, and there are few parallels to his long fight to bring the benefits of low-cost electricity to the people of the Tennessee Valley, although they lived a thousand miles from his home state of Nebraska. But there were three struggles in his life that are worthy of especial note for the courage displayed—the overthrow of "Czar" Cannon already described; his support of Al Smith for President in 1928; and his filibuster against the Armed Ship Bill in 1917.

* * *

When Woodrow Wilson, sorrowfully determined upon a policy of "armed neutrality" in early 1917, appeared before a tense joint session of Congress to request legislation authorizing him to arm American merchant ships, the American public gave its immediate approval. Unrestricted German submarine warfare was enforcing a tight blockade by which the Kaiser sought to starve the British Isles into submission; and Secretary of State Lansing had been politely informed that every American ship encountered in the war zone would be torpedoed. Already American vessels had been searched, seized and sunk. Tales of atrocities to our seamen filled the press.

As debate on the bill got under way, the newspapers learned of a new plot against the United States, contained in a message from the German Under Secretary of State for Foreign Affairs, Zimmerman, to the German Minister in Mexico. The alleged note (for there were those who questioned its authenticity and the motives of the British and American governments in disclosing it at that particular time) proposed a scheme to align Mexico and Japan against the United States. In return for its use as an invasion base, Mexico was promised restoration of her "American colonies," seized more than seventy years earlier by Sam Houston and his compatriots.

When the contents of the Zimmerman note were leaked to the newspapers, all resistance to the Armed Ship Bill in the House of Representatives instantly collapsed. The bill was rushed through that body by the overwhelming vote of 403 to 13—a vote which seemed clearly representative of popular opinion in favor of the President's move. Certainly the overwhelming support given the bill by Nebraska's Congressmen represented the feelings of that state.

But in the Senate on March 2, 1917, the Armed Ship Bill met determined opposition from a small bipartisan band of insurgents led by Robert La Follette of Wisconsin and George Norris of Nebraska. As freshman Senator from a state which the previous year had voted for a Democratic legislature, Governor, Senator and President, George Norris (unlike La Follette) was neither a solidly established political figure in his own bailiwick nor confident that his people were opposed to Wilson and his policies.

In previous months he had supported the President on major foreign policy issues, including the severing of diplomatic ties with the German government. Although a militant pacifist and isolationist, his very nature prohibited him from being a mere obstructionist on all international issues, or a petty partisan opposing all of the President's requests. (Indeed, by the time World War II approached, his isolationism had largely vanished.)

But George Norris hated war—and he feared that "Big Business," which he believed was providing the stimuli for our progress along the road to war, was bent on driving the nation into a useless, bloody struggle; that the President—far from taking the people into his confidence—was trying to stampede public opinion into pressuring the Senate for war; and that the Armed Ship Bill was a device to protect American munition profits with American lives, a device which could push us directly into the conflict as a combatant without further deliberation by Congress or actual attack upon the United States by Germany. He was fearful of the bill's broad grant of authority, and he was resentful of the manner in which it was being steamrollered through the Congress. It is not now important whether Norris was right or wrong. What is now important is the courage he displayed in support of his convictions.

"People may not believe it," Senator Norris once said, "but I don't like to get into fights." In 1917, whether he liked it or not, the freshman from Nebraska prepared for one of the hardest, most embittering struggles of his political career. Since those days were prior to Norris' own Twentieth, or Lame Duck, Amendment, the Sixty-fourth Congress would expire at noon of March 4, when a new Presidential term began. Thus passage of the bill by that Congress could be prevented if the Senate could not vote before that hour; and Norris and his little band were hopeful that the new Congress, chosen by the people during the Presidential campaign of 1916—based upon the slogan "He kept us out of war"—might join in opposition to the measure, or at least give it more careful consideration. But preventing a vote during the next two days spelled only one word—filibuster!

George Norris, an advocate of a change in the Senate rules to correct the abuses of filibustering, but feeling strongly that the issue of war itself was at stake, adopted this very tactic "in spite of my repugnance to the method." As parliamentary floor leader for his group, he arranged speakers to make certain that there was no possibility of a break in the debate which would enable the bill to come to a vote.

Many of his closest friends in the Senate were aghast at this conduct. "No state but one populated by molly-coddles," complained one Senator well aware of the raging anti-German sentiment back home, "would endorse what Norris is trying to do." But Nebraska did *not* endorse the position of its junior Senator. As debate got under way, the Nebraska newspapers, in a thinly veiled warning, reported that the tremendous vote in the House "represents the sentiments of the people." And the Nebraska Legislature had already unanimously pledged to President Wilson "the loyal and undivided support of the entire citizenry of the state of Nebraska, of whatever political party and of whatever blood or place of birth, in whatever may be found necessary to maintain the right of Americans, the dignity of our nation and the honor of our flag."

But George Norris' guide was his own conscience. "Otherwise," he said, "a member of Congress giving weight to expressed public sentiment becomes only an automatic machine, and Congress requires no patriotism, no education, and no courage. . . ." And so, with only his conscience to sustain him, the Senator worked around the clock to bolster the sagging spirits of his little band, to prepare new speakers for continuous debate and to check every opposition move to end the filibuster.

Several Senators, Norris later related, privately approached him to wish the filibuster success, while pleading party regularity and political expediency as their grounds for publicly supporting the President's position. When Norris told them that the important thing was to make certain there were plenty of speakers, regardless of the views expressed, two of the President's supporters, by private agreement with Norris, spoke at length in favor of the bill.

Day and night the debate continued; and on the morning of March 4 the Senate was a scene of weary disorder. "Those final minutes," Norris later wrote, "live in my memory."

In that chamber, men became slaves to emotion. The clash of anger and bitterness, in my judgment, never has been exceeded in the history of the United States. When the hour hand pointed to the arrival of noon, the chairman announced adjournment. The filibuster had won. The conference report which would have authorized the arming of American ships had failed of Senate approval. . . . Tense excitement prevailed throughout the entire country, and especially in the Senate itself. . . . I have felt from that day to this the filibuster was justified. I never have apologized for the part I took in it. . . . [We] honestly believed that, by our actions in that struggle, we had averted American participation in the war.

But theirs was a fleeting victory. For the President—in addition to immediately calling a special session of Congress in which the Senate adopted a closure rule to limit debate (with Norris' support)—also announced that a further examination of the statutes had revealed that the executive power already included the right to arm ships without Congressional action. And the President also let loose a blast, still frequently quoted today, against "a little group of willful men, representing no opinion but their own, that rendered the great government of the United States helpless and contemptible."

George Norris called the President's scathing indictment a grave injustice to men who conscientiously tried to do their duty as they saw it; but, except for the unfortunate and unhelpful praise bestowed upon them by the German press, "the epithets heaped upon these men were without precedent in the annals of American journalism." They had earned, in the words of the Louisville *Courier Journal*, "an eternity of execration." A mass meeting at Carnegie Hall condemned Norris and his colleagues as "treasonable and reprehensible" men "who refused to defend the Stars and Stripes on the high seas"; and the crowd hooted "traitor" and "hang him" whenever the names of Norris, La Follette and their supporters were mentioned. "The time has come," the Mayor of New York shouted to another meeting, "when the people of this country are to be divided into two classes—Americans and traitors."

The Hartford *Courant* called them "political tramps," and the New York *Sun* labeled twelve United States Senators "a group of moral perverts." The Providence *Journal* called their action "little short of treason" and the *New York Times* editorialized that "The odium of treasonable purpose will rest upon their names forevermore." The New York *Herald* predicted: "They will be fortunate if their names do not go down into history bracketed with that of Benedict Arnold."

In the decades to follow, Senator Norris would learn to withstand the merciless abuse inevitably heaped upon one of his independent and outspoken views. On the Senate floor itself, he would be called a Bolshevist, an enemy of advancement, a traitor and much more. But now the harsh terms of vilification and the desertion of former friends hurt him deeply. One afternoon several passengers left a Washington trolley car when Norris and La Follette took seats beside them. His mail was abusive, several letters containing sketches showing him in German uniform complete with medals.

The Nebraska press joined in the denunciation of its junior Senator. "Can Senator Norris believe," cried the Omaha *World Herald* (which had listed on page 1 the names of "Twelve Senators Who Halt Action in Greatest Crisis Since Civil War"), "can any man in his senses believe, that the American Government could tamely submit to these outrages?"

"The Norris fear of the establishment of an absolute monarchy under Wilson is grotesque," said the Lincoln *Star*. "Maybe it is a joke. If not, friends of Mr. Norris should look after his mental status." And the Omaha *Bee* thought his fear of Presidential authority "reflects little credit on the Senator's common sense."

It was believed in Washington that the conscience of the freshman from Nebraska had led him, in the words of one Washington correspondent, to "his political death." The outraged Nebraska State Legislature, with whooping enthusiasm, passed a resolution expressing the confidence of the state in President Wilson and his policies.

George Norris was saddened by the near unanimity with which "my own people condemned me . . . and asserted that I was misrepresenting my state." Although popularity was not his standard, he had tried, he later wrote, throughout his career "to do what in my own heart I believed to be right for the people at large." Thus, unwilling to "represent the people of Nebraska if they did not want me," he came to a dramatic decision—he would offer to resign from the Senate and submit to a special recall election, "to let my constituents decide whether I was representing them or misrepresenting them in Washington." In letters to the Governor and the Republican State Chairman, he urged a special election, agreeing to abide by the result and to waive whatever constitutional rights protected him from recall.

Sharing the fears of his astonished friends in the Senate that hysteria and well-financed opposition might insure his defeat which in turn would be interpreted as a mandate for war, he nevertheless insisted in his letter to the Governor that he had "no desire to represent the people of Nebraska if my official conduct is contrary to their wishes."

> The denunciation I have received . . . indicates to me that there is strong probability that the course I have pursued is unsatisfactory to the people whom I represent, and it seems, therefore, only fair that the matter should be submitted to them for decision.
>
> I will not, however, even at the behest of a unanimous constituency, violate my oath of office by voting in favor of a proposition that means the surrender by Congress of its sole right to declare war. . . . If my refusal to do this is contrary to the wishes of the people of Nebraska, then I should be recalled and someone else selected to fill the place. . . . I am, however, so firmly convinced of the righteousness of my course that I believe if the intelligent and patriotic citizenship of the country can only have an opportunity to hear both sides of the question, all the money in Christendom and all the political machinery that wealth can congregate will not be able to defeat the principle of government for which our forefathers fought. . . . If I am wrong, then I not only ought to retire, but I desire to do so. I have no desire to hold public office if I am expected blindly to follow in my official actions the dictation of a newspaper combination . . . or be a rubber stamp even for the President of the United States.

The Senator, announcing an open meeting in Lincoln to explain his position, was largely ignored by the press as he journeyed homeward. Attempting to get the Republican National Committeeman to act as chairman of the meeting, he was warned by that worthy gentleman that it was "not possible for this meeting to be held without trouble. I think the meeting will be broken up or at least you will have such an unfriendly audience that it will be impossible for you to make any coherent speech." One of the few friends who called upon him urged him to cancel the meeting by pleading illness, telling Norris that he had made a very sad mistake in returning to Nebraska when feelings ran so high. Others predicted that agitators would be scattered throughout the audience to make presentation of his arguments impossible, and told the Senator that the torpedoing of three more American merchant ships since the filibuster had further intensified the anger of his constituents. "I cannot remember a day in my life," the Senator wrote in his autobiography, "when I have suffered more from a lonely feeling of despondency. My friends led me to believe that the people of Nebraska were almost unanimously against me."

Unable to get a single friend or supporter to act as chairman, Norris was nevertheless determined to go through with the meeting. "I myself hired the hall," he told a lonely reporter in his deserted hotel room, "and it is to be my meeting. I am asking no one to stand sponsor for me or for my acts. But I have nothing to apologize for and nothing to take back."

Walking from his hotel to the city auditorium on a beautiful spring night, Norris anxiously noted that more than three thousand people—the concerned, the skeptical and the curious—had filled the auditorium, with many standing in the aisles and outside in the street. Calm but trembling, he walked out on the stage before them and stood for a moment without speaking, a solitary figure in a baggy black suit and a little shoestring tie. "I had expected an unfriendly audience," he wrote, "and it was with some fear that I stepped forward. When I entered the rear of the auditorium and stepped out on the stage, there was a deathlike silence. There was not a single handclap. But I had not expected applause; and I was delighted that I was not hissed."

In his homely, quiet, and yet intense manner, Senator Norris began with the simple phrase: "I have come home to tell you the truth."

> Immediately there was a burst of applause from all parts of the audience. Never in my lifetime has applause done me the good that did. . . . There was, in the hearts of the common people, a belief that underneath the deception and the misrepresentation, the political power and the influence, there was something artificial about the propaganda.

There was no violence, there was no heckling; and the tremendous crowd cheered mightily as Norris lashed out at his critics. His dry, simple but persistent language and the quiet intensity of his anger captivated his audience, as he insisted that their newspapers were not giving them the facts and that, despite warnings that he stay away until his role in the filibuster was forgotten, he wanted it to be remembered. More than half of the New York audience which had hissed him had been in evening dress, he sarcastically recalled, and he questioned how many of them were willing to fight or send their children:

> Of course, if poodledogs could have been made into soldiers that audience would have supplied a regiment. . . . My colleague talked two and a half hours for the bill and was called a hero. I talked one hour and a half against the bill and was called a traitor. Even though you say I am wrong, even though you feel sure I should have stood by the President, has the time come when we can't even express our opinions in the Senate, where we were sent to debate such questions, without being branded by the moneyed interests as traitors? I can stand up and take my medicine

without wincing under any charge except that of traitor. In all of the English language, in all the tongues of the world, you can't find any other words as damnable as that.

The crowd, after more than an hour, roared its approval. The newspapers were not so easily convinced or so willing to forgive. "His elaborate and ingenious explanation," said the *World Herald*, is "foolish nonsense . . . a silly statement, which has disgusted the people." "The Senator spent little time meeting the issue as it actually stood," said the *State Journal*. "He should not let his critics disturb his balance."

But Senator Norris, who was asked to appear before many groups to explain what he felt to be the true issues, met acclaim throughout the state; and the Governor having announced that he would not ask the Legislature to authorize a special recall election, the Senator returned to Washington better able to withstand the abuse which had not yet fully ceased.

* * *

During the next eleven years George Norris' fame and political fortune multiplied. In 1928, despite his continued differences with the Republican party and its administrations, the Nebraska Senator was one of the party's most prominent members, Chairman of the Senate Judiciary Committee and a potential Presidential nominee. But Norris himself scoffed at the latter reports:

I have no expectation of being nominated for President. A man who has followed the political course I have is barred from the office. . . . I realize perfectly that no man holding the views I do is going to be nominated for the Presidency.

With an oath he rejected the suggestion that he accept a position as Herbert Hoover's running mate, and he attacked the Republican Convention's platform and the methods by which it had selected its nominees. In those years prior to the establishment of the T.V.A., the Senator from Nebraska was the nation's most outspoken advocate of public power; and he believed that the "monopolistic power trust" had dictated the nomination of Hoover and the Republican platform.

Unwilling to commit himself to the Democratic party he had always opposed, and whose platform he believed to be equally weak, Norris toured the country campaigning for fellow progressives regardless of party. But as the campaign utterances of Democratic nominee Al Smith of New York began to fall into line with Norris' own views, he was confronted with the most difficult political problem of his career.

George Norris was a Republican, a Midwesterner, a Protestant and a "dry," and Herbert Hoover was all of those things. But Al Smith—a Tammany Hall Democrat from the streets of New York, and a Catholic who favored the repeal of Prohibition—was none of them. Surely Smith could have little support in Nebraska, which was also Republican, Midwestern, Protestant and dry by nature. Could Norris possibly desert his party, his state and his constituents under such circumstances?

He could. He had always maintained that he "would like to abolish party responsibility and in its stead establish personal responsibility. Any man even though he be the strictest kind of Republican, who does not believe the things I stand for are right, should follow his convictions and vote against me." And thus in 1928 Norris finally declared that progressives

> had no place to land except in the Smith camp. . . . Shall we be so partisan that we will place our party above our country and refuse to follow the only leader who affords us any escape from the control of the [power] trust? . . . It seems to me we cannot crush our consciences and support somebody who we know in advance is opposed to the very things for which we have been fighting so many years.

But what about Smith's religious views? What about his attitude on the liquor question?

> It is possible for a man in public life to separate his religious beliefs from his political activities. . . . I am a Protestant and a dry, yet I would support a man who was a wet and a Catholic provided I believed he was sincerely in favor of law enforcement and was right on economic issues. . . . I'd rather trust an honest wet who is progressive and courageous in his makeup than politicians who profess to be on the dry side but do no more to make prohibition effective than all the rum runners and bootleggers in the country.

These were courageous sentiments, but they were lost on an indignant constituency. As his train sped through the state on the way to Omaha, where he was to speak for Smith over a nationwide radio hookup, long-time friends and Republican leaders climbed aboard to appeal in the name of his party and career. The head of the powerful Nebraska Anti-Saloon League, previously an important supporter of Norris, termed his injection of the power issue poppycock. "The issue in this campaign is the liquor issue and Norris knows it. If he makes this speech for Smith, the League is through with him." (Norris, when asked if he would run for re-election in 1930 in view of such statements, dryly replied that "such things might drive me to it.") The pastor of the largest Baptist church in Omaha wrote the Senator that he did not "represent us at all, and we are very much ashamed of your attitude toward the administration." But Norris, in his reply, calmly asked the minister whether he had "made any attempt to take the beam out of your own eyes, so that you can see more clearly how to pluck the mote out of your brother's eye."

Old Guard Republican leaders had previously insisted, at least privately, that Norris was "no Republican," a charge they now made openly. But now many of Norris' most devoted followers expressed dismay at his bolt. Said an Eagle, Nebraska, small businessman: "I have supported Norris for 20 years, but never again. He is politically warped and mentally a grouch, and has antagonized every Republican administration since Roosevelt. The Senator should have more respect for his admirers than to expect them to cast their lot with a wet Democrat." Norris' first Congressional secretary told reporters he was "bitterly opposed to the Senator's unwarranted support of Tammany's candidate for President."

A delegate who had supported Norris for President at the Republican Convention told the press that Norris "does not carry my political conscience in his vest pocket. I am deeply grieved to see the stand he has taken. Norris should seek new friends, and if he chooses to find them on the sidewalks of New York that is his privilege. But it is unfortunate that he uses the Republican party as a vehicle to ride into office and then repudiates its standard-bearer."

The editor of the Walthill *Times* wrote: "I say it sadly, but I am through with Norris. Politically he is lost in the wilderness, far away from his old progressive friends."

"For a hungry farmer or a thirsty wet of less than average political judgment," said a Lincoln attorney who was close to the Norris camp, "there may be an excuse. But for a statesman of Norris' ability and experience there is no excuse."

But George Norris sought to help the hungry farmer even if it meant helping the thirsty wet. Unmoved by either appeals or attacks, he delivered a powerful plea for Smith at Omaha. The New York Governor, he said, had risen above the dictates of Tammany, while the techniques employed by the Republican Convention would "make Tammany Hall appear as a white-robed saint." He was "traveling in very distinguished company" by supporting the candidate of the opposing party, he told his audience, for Herbert Hoover himself had acted similarly ten years earlier. But for the most part his speech was an attack on the power trust, "an octopus with slimy fingers that levies tribute upon every fireside," and upon Hoover's refusal to discuss these questions: "to sin by silence when we should protest makes cowards out of men."

Finally, Norris closed his address by meeting the religious issue openly:

> It is our duty as patriots to cast out this Un-American doctrine and rebuke those who have raised the torch of intolerance. All believers of any faith can unite and go forward in our political work to bring about the maximum amount of happiness for our people.

But in 1928 the people of Nebraska were not willing to listen to the theme of tolerance or a discussion of the issues. Telegrams poured in attacking Norris for his support of a Catholic and a wet. "The storm which followed that Omaha pronouncement for Smith," Norris later recalled, "was more violent than any I had ever encountered. It was well that I had had some training in the matter of abuse." Even his wife was quoted by the papers as saying she would vote for neither Smith nor Hoover: "I am not following George in all this. . . . I have always been a dry and I am not going to vote for Smith even if George does." Although the same powerful Democratic newspaper, the Omaha *World Herald*, which had assailed his stand for principle against Woodrow Wilson, was now able to applaud Senator Norris "for his splendid courage and devotion," other Nebraska newspapers accused him of deserting his state for Tammany Hall in the hopes of reviving his own Presidential boom four years later. His speech had endangered the chances for re-election of his own liberal Republican colleague, and his fellow insurgent Republicans in the Senate expressed their disapproval of his course. When the Senator returned to his home town he found his friends and other leading citizens turning away, as though they would be glad to "cut my heart out and hang it on a fence as a warning to others."

The landslide for Hoover, who carried practically every county and community in Nebraska, as well as the country as a whole, embittered Norris, who declared that Hoover had won on the false questions of religion and prohibition, when the real problems were power and farm relief. The special interests and machine politicians, he said, "kept this issue to the front [although] they knew it was a false, wicked and unfair issue."

* * *

George Norris' filibuster against the Armed Ship Bill had failed, both in its immediate goal of preventing the President's action, and in its attempt to keep the nation out of the war into which it was plunged a few months later. His campaign for Al Smith also failed, and failed dismally. And yet, as the Senator confided to a friend in later years:

> It happens very often that one tries to do something and fails. He feels discouraged, and yet he may discover years afterward that the very effort he made was the reason why somebody else took it up and succeeded. I really believe that whatever use I have been to progressive civilization has been accomplished in the things I failed to do than in the things I actually did do.

George Norris met with both success and failure in his long tenure in public office, stretching over nearly a half a century of American political life. But the essence of the man and his career was caught in a tribute paid to the Republican Senator from Nebraska by the Democratic Presidential nominee in September, 1932:

> History asks, "Did the man have integrity?
> Did the man have unselfishness?
> Did the man have courage?
> Did the man have consistency?"
>
> There are few statesmen in America today who so definitely and clearly measure up to an affirmative answer to those four questions as does George W. Norris.

IX

ROBERT A. TAFT

". . . LIBERTY OF THE INDIVIDUAL TO THINK HIS OWN THOUGHTS . . ."

The late Senator Robert A. Taft of Ohio was never President of the United States. Therein lies his personal tragedy. And therein lies his national greatness.

For the Presidency was a goal that Bob Taft pursued throughout his career in the Senate, an ambition that this son of a former President always dreamed of realizing. As the leading exponent of the Republican philosophy for more than a decade, "Mr. Republican" was bitterly disappointed by his failure on three different occasions even to receive the nomination.

But Robert A. Taft was also a man who stuck fast to the basic principles in which he believed—and when those fundamental principles were at issue, not even the lure of the White House, or the possibilities of injuring his candidacy, could deter him from speaking out. He was an able politician, but on more than one occasion he chose to speak out in defense of a position no politician with like ambitions would have endorsed. He was, moreover, a brilliant political analyst, who knew that during his lifetime the number of American voters who agreed with the fundamental tenets of his political philosophy was destined to be a permanent minority, and that only by flattering new blocs of support—while carefully refraining from alienating any group which contained potential Taft voters—could he ever hope to attain his goal. Yet he frequently flung to the winds the very restraints his own analysis advised, refusing to bow to any group, refusing to keep silent on any issue.

It is not that Bob Taft's career in the Senate was a constant battle between popularity and principle as was John Quincy Adams'; he did not have to struggle to maintain his integrity like Thomas Hart Benton. His principles usually led him to conclusions which a substantial percentage of his constituents and political associates were willing to support. Although on occasions his political conduct reflected his political ambitions, popularity was not his guide on most fundamental matters. The Taft-Hartley Labor Management Relations Act could not have gained him many votes in industrialized Ohio, for those who endorsed its curbs on union activity were already Taft supporters; but it brought furious anti-Taft reprisals during the 1950 Senate campaign by the unions in Ohio, and it nourished the belief that Taft could not win a Presidential contest, a belief which affected his chances for the nomination in 1952. Simultaneously, however, he was antagonizing the friends of Taft-Hartley, and endangering his own leadership in the Republican party, by his support of education, housing, health and other welfare measures.

Those who were shocked at these apparent departures from his traditional position did not comprehend that Taft's conservatism contained a strong strain of pragmatism, which caused him to support intensive Federal activity in those areas that he believed not adequately served by the private enterprise system. Taft did not believe that this was inconsistent with the conservative doctrine; conservatism in his opinion was not irresponsibility. Thus he gave new dimensions to the conservative philosophy: he stuck to that faith when it reached its lowest depth of prestige and power and led it back to the level of responsibility and respectability. He was an unusual leader, for he lacked the fine arts of oratory and phrasemaking, he lacked blind devotion to the party line (unless he dictated it), and he lacked the politician's natural instinct to avoid controversial positions and issues.

But he was more than a political leader, more than "Mr. Republican." He was also a Taft—and thus "Mr. Integrity." The Senator's grandfather, Alphonso Taft, had moved West to practice law in 1830, writing his father that "The notorious selfishness and dishonesty of the great mass of men you find in New York is to my mind a serious obstacle to settling there." And the Senator's father was William Howard Taft, who knew well the meaning of political courage and political abuse when he stood by his Secretary of Interior, Ballinger, against the overwhelming opposition of Pinchot, Roosevelt and the progressive elements of his own party.

So Bob Taft, as his biographer has described it, was "born to integrity." He was known in the Senate as a man who never broke an agreement, who never compromised his deeply felt Republican principles, who never practiced political deception. His bitter political enemy, Harry Truman, would say when the Senator died: "He and I did not agree on public policy, but he knew where I stood and I knew where he stood. We need intellectually honest men like Senator Taft." Examples of his candor are endless and startling. The Ohioan once told a group in the heart of Republican farm territory that farm prices were too high; and he told still another farm group that "he was tired of seeing all these people riding in Cadillacs." His support of an extensive Federal housing program caused a colleague to remark: "I hear the Socialists have gotten to Bob Taft." He informed an important political associate who cherished a commendatory message signed by Taft that his assistant "sent those things out by the dozen" without the Senator even seeing, much less signing them. And a colleague recalls that he did not reject the ideas of his friends by gentle indirection, but by coldly and unhesitatingly terming them "nonsense." "He had," as William S. White has written, "a luminous candor of purpose that was extraordinarily refreshing in a chamber not altogether devoted to candor."

It would be a mistake, however, to conclude from this that Senator Taft was cold and abrupt in his personal relationships. I recall, from my own very brief service with him in the Senate and on the Senate Labor Committee in the last months of his life, my strong impression of a surprising and unusual personal charm, and a disarming simplicity of manner. It was these qualities, combined with an unflinching courage which he exhibited throughout his entire life and most especially in his last days, that bound his adherents to him with unbreakable ties.

Perhaps we are as yet too close in time to the controversial elements in the career of Senator Taft to be able to measure his life with historical perspective. A man who can inspire intensely bitter enemies as well as intensely devoted followers is best judged after many years pass, enough years to permit the sediment of political and legislative battles to settle, so that we can assess our times more clearly.

But sufficient time has passed since 1946 to enable something of a detached view of Senator Taft's act of courage in that year. Unlike the acts of Daniel Webster or Edmund Ross, it did not change history. Unlike those of John Quincy Adams, or Thomas Benton, it did not bring about his retirement from the Senate. Unlike most of those deeds of courage previously described, it did not even take place on the Senate floor. But as a piece of sheer candor in a period when candor was out of favor, as a bold plea for justice in a time of intolerance and hostility, it is worth remembering here.

* * *

In October of 1946, Senator Robert A. Taft of Ohio was the chief spokesman for the Republicans in Washington, the champion of his party in the national political arena and the likely Republican nominee for the Presidency in 1948. It was a time when even a Senator with such an established reputation for speaking his mind would have guarded his tongue, and particularly a Senator with so much at stake as Bob Taft. The party which had been his whole life, the Republicans of the Congress for whom he spoke, now once again were nearing the brink of success in the fall elections. Capturing for his party control of both Houses of Congress would enhance Bob Taft's prestige, reinforce his right to the Republican Presidential nomination and pave the way for his triumphant return to the White House from which his father had been somewhat ingloriously ousted in 1912. Or so it seemed to most political observers at the time, who assumed the Republican leader would say nothing to upset the applecart. With Congress out of session, with the tide running strongly against the incumbent Democrats, there appeared to be no necessity for the Senator to make more than the usual campaign utterances on the usual issues.

But Senator Taft was disturbed—and when he was disturbed it was his habit to speak out. He was disturbed by the War Crimes Trials of Axis leaders, then concluding in Germany and about to commence in Japan. The Nuremberg Trials, in which eleven notorious Nazis had been found guilty under an impressively documented indictment for "waging an aggressive war," had been popular throughout the world and particularly in the United States. Equally popular was the sentence already announced by the high tribunal: death.

But what kind of trial was this? "No matter how many books are written or briefs filed," Supreme Court Justice William O. Douglas has recently written, "no matter how finely the lawyers analyzed it, the crime for which the Nazis were tried had never been formalized as a crime with the definiteness required by our legal standards, nor outlawed with a death penalty by the international community. By our standards that crime arose under an *ex post facto* law. Goering et al deserved severe punishment. But their guilt did not justify us in substituting power for principle."

These conclusions are shared, I believe, by a substantial number of American citizens today. And they were shared, at least privately, by a goodly number in 1946. But no politician of consequence would speak out —certainly not after the verdict had already been announced and preparations for the executions were already under way—none, that is, but Senator Taft.

The Constitution of the United States was the gospel which guided the policy decisions of the Senator from Ohio. It was his source, his weapon and his salvation. And when the Constitution commanded no "*ex post facto* laws," Bob Taft accepted this precept as permanently wise and universally applicable. The Constitution was not a collection of loosely given political promises subject to broad interpretation. It was not a list of pleasing platitudes to be set lightly aside when expediency required it. It was the foundation of the American system of law and justice and he was repelled by the picture of his country discarding those Constitutional precepts in order to punish a vanquished enemy.

Still, why should he say anything? The Nuremberg Trials were at no time before the Congress for consideration. They were not in any sense an issue in the campaign. There was no Republican or Democratic position on a matter enthusiastically applauded by the entire nation. And no speech by any United States Senator, however powerful, could prevent the death sentence from being carried out. To speak out unnecessarily would be politically costly and clearly futile.

But Bob Taft spoke out.

On October 6, 1946, Senator Taft appeared before a conference on our Anglo-American heritage, sponsored by Kenyon College in Ohio. The war crimes trial was not an issue upon which conference speakers were expected to comment. But titling his address "Equal Justice Under Law" Taft cast aside his general reluctance to embark upon startlingly novel and dramatic approaches. "The trial of the vanquished by the victors," he told an attentive if somewhat astonished audience, "cannot be impartial no matter how it is hedged about with the forms of justice."

> I question whether the hanging of those, who, however despicable, were the leaders of the German people, will ever discourage the making of aggressive war, for no one makes aggressive war unless he expects to win. About this whole judgment there is the spirit of vengeance, and vengeance is seldom justice. The hanging of the eleven men convicted will be a blot on the American record which we shall long regret.
>
> In these trials we have accepted the Russian idea of the purpose of trials—government policy and not justice—with little relation to Anglo-Saxon heritage. By clothing policy in the forms of legal procedure, we may discredit the whole idea of justice in Europe for years to come. In the last analysis, even at the end of a frightful war, we should view the future with more hope if even our enemies believed that we had treated them justly in our English-speaking concept of law, in the provision of relief and in the final disposal of territory.

In ten days the Nazi leaders were to be hanged. But Bob Taft, speaking in cold, clipped matter-of-fact tones, deplored that sentence, and suggested that involuntary exile—similar to that imposed upon Napoleon—might be wiser. But even more deplorable, he said, were the trials themselves, which "violate the fundamental principle of American law that a man cannot be tried under an *ex post facto* statute." Nuremberg, the Ohio Senator insisted, was a blot on American Constitutional history, and a serious departure from our Anglo-Saxon heritage of fair and equal treatment, a heritage which had rightly made this country respected throughout the world. "We can't even teach our own people the sound principles of liberty and justice," he concluded. "We cannot teach them government in Germany by suppressing liberty and justice. As I see it, the English-speaking peoples have one great responsibility. That is to restore to the minds of men a devotion to equal justice under law."

The speech exploded in the midst of a heated election campaign; and throughout the nation Republican candidates scurried for shelter while Democrats seized the opportunity to advance. Many, many people were outraged at Taft's remarks. Those who had fought, or whose men had fought and possibly died, to beat back the German aggressors were contemptuous of these fine phrases by a politician who had never seen battle. Those whose kinsmen or former countrymen had been among the Jews, Poles, Czechs and other nationality groups terrorized by Hitler and his cohorts were shocked. The memories of the gas chambers at Buchenwald and other Nazi concentration camps, the stories of hideous atrocities which had been refreshed with new illustrations at Nuremberg, and the anguish and suffering which each new military casualty list had brought to thousands of American homes—these were among the immeasurable influences which caused many to react with pain and indignation when a United States Senator deplored the trials and sentences of these merely "despicable" men.

In New York, the most important state in any Presidential race, and a state where politics were particularly sensitive to the views of various nationality and minority groups, Democrats were joyous and Republicans angry and gloomy. The 1944 Republican Presidential nominee, and Taft's bitter rival for party control and the 1948 nomination, New York's Governor Thomas E. Dewey, declared that the verdicts were justified; and in a statement in which the New York Republican nominee for the Senate, Irving Ives, joined, he stated: "The defendants at Nuremberg had a fair and extensive trial. *No one* can have any sympathy for these Nazi leaders who brought such agony upon the world." The Democratic State Campaign Manager in New York challenged Taft "to come into this state and repeat his plea for the lives of the Nazi war criminals."

The Democratic Party has a perfect right to ask if the public wants the type of national administration, or state administration, favored by Senator Taft, who indicated he wants the lives of the convicted Nazis spared and who may very well be preparing the way for a Republican propaganda campaign to commute the death sentences of the Nazi murderers.

New York Republican Congressional candidate Jacob K. Javits sent a telegram to Taft calling his statement "a disservice to all we fought for and to the cause of future peace." The Democratic nominee for United States Senator in New York expressed his deep shock at the Taft statement and his certainty it would be repudiated by "right-thinking and fair-minded Americans." And the Democratic nominee for Governor told his audiences that if Senator Taft had ever seen the victims of Nazi concentration camps, he never would have been able to make such a statement.

Even in the nation's Capital, where Taft was greatly admired and his blunt candor was more or less expected, the reaction was no different. G.O.P. leaders generally declined official comment, but privately expressed their fears over the consequences for their Congressional candidates. At a press conference, the Chairman of the

Republican Congressional Campaign Committee refused to comment on the subject, stating that he had "his own ideas" on the Nuremberg trials but did not "wish to enter into a controversy with Senator Taft."

The Democrats, however, were jubilant—although concealing their glee behind a façade of shocked indignation. At his weekly press conference, President Truman smilingly suggested he would be glad to let Senator Taft and Governor Dewey fight the matter out. Democratic Majority Leader in the Senate (and later Vice President) Alben Barkley of Kentucky told a campaign audience that Taft "never experienced a crescendo of heart about the soup kitchens of 1932, but his heart bled anguishedly for the criminals at Nuremberg." Typical of Democratic reaction was the statement of Senator Scott Lucas of Illinois, who called Taft's speech "a classical example of his muddled and confused thinking" and predicted it would "boomerang on his aspirations for the Presidential nomination of 1948."

> 11,000,000 fighting veterans of World War II will answer Mr. Taft. . . . I doubt that the Republican National Chairman will permit the Senator to make any more speeches now that Taft has called the trials a blot on the American record. . . . Neither the American people nor history will agree. . . . Senator Taft, whether he believed it or not, was defending these culprits who were responsible for the murder of ten million people.

Even in Taft's home bailiwick of Ohio, where his strict constitutionalism had won him immense popularity, the Senator's speech brought anger, confusion and political reverberations. The Republican Senatorial candidate, former Governor John Bricker, was not only a close ally of Taft but had been the Vice Presidential nominee in 1944 as running mate to Governor Dewey. His Democratic opponent, incumbent Senator James Huffman, challenged Bricker to stand with either Taft or Dewey, declaring:

> A country that has suffered the scourge of modern war, lost more than 300,000 of its finest men, and spent $300,000,000,000 of its resources because of the acts of these convicted gangsters can never feel that the sentences meted out have been too severe. . . . This is not the time to weaken in the punishment of international crimes. Such criticism, even if justified, should have been offered when the international tribunals were being set up.

The Toledo *Blade* told its readers that "on this issue, as on so many others, Senator Taft shows that he has a wonderful mind which knows practically everything and understands practically nothing. . . ."

The Cleveland *Plain Dealer* editorialized that Taft "may be technically correct," but turning "loose on the world the worst gang of cutthroats in all history . . . would have failed to give the world that great principle which humanity needs so desperately to have established: the principle that planning and waging aggressive war is definitely a crime against humanity."

Senator Taft was disheartened by the voracity of his critics—and extremely uncomfortable when one of the acquitted Nazi leaders, Franz Von Papen, told interviewers upon his release from prison that he agreed with Taft's speech. A spokesman for Taft issued only one terse statement: "He has stated his feeling on the matter and feels that if others want to criticize him, let them go ahead." But the Ohio Senator could not understand why even his old supporter, newspaper columnist David Lawrence, called his position nothing more than a "technical quibble." And he must have been particularly distressed when respected Constitutional authorities such as the President of the American Bar Association, the Chairman of its Executive Committee and other leading members of the legal profession all deplored his statement and defended the trials as being in accordance with international law.

For Robert Taft had spoken, not in "defense of the Nazi murderers" (as a labor leader charged), not in defense of isolationism (as most observers assumed), but in defense of what he regarded to be the traditional American concepts of law and justice. As the apostle of strict constitutionalism, as the chief defense attorney for the conservative way of life and government, Robert Alphonso Taft was undeterred by the possibilities of injury to his party's precarious position or his own Presidential prospects. To him, justice was at stake, and all other concerns were trivial. "It illustrates at once," a columnist observed at that time, "the extreme stubbornness, integrity and political strongheadedness of Senator Taft."

> The fact that thousands disagree with him, and that it is politically embarrassing to other Republicans, probably did not bother Taft at all. He has for years been accustomed to making up his mind, regardless of whether it hurts him or anyone else. Taft surely must have known that his remarks would be twisted and misconstrued and that his timing would raise the devil in the current campaign. But it is characteristic of him that he went ahead anyway.

The storm raised by his speech eventually died down. It did not, after all the uproar, appear to affect the Republican sweep in 1946, nor was it—at least openly—an issue in Taft's drive for the Presidential nomination in 1948. The Nazi leaders were hanged, and Taft and the country went on to other matters. But we are not concerned today with the question of whether Taft was right or wrong in his condemnation of the Nuremberg trials. What is noteworthy is the illustration furnished by this speech of Taft's unhesitating courage in standing against the flow of public opinion for a cause he believed to be right. His action was characteristic of the man who was labeled a reactionary, who was proud to be a conservative and who authored these lasting definitions of liberalism and liberty:

> Liberalism implies particularly freedom of thought, freedom from orthodox dogma, the right of others to think

differently from one's self. It implies a free mind, open to new ideas and willing to give attentive consideration. . . .

When I say liberty, I mean liberty of the individual to think his own thoughts and live his own life as he desires to think and live.

This was the creed by which Senator Taft lived, and he sought in his own fashion and in his own way to provide an atmosphere in America in which others could do likewise.

X

OTHER MEN OF POLITICAL COURAGE

". . . Consolation . . . for the Contempt of Mankind."

There is no official "list" of politically courageous Senators, and it has not been my intention to suggest one. On the contrary, by retelling *some* of the most outstanding and dramatic stories of political courage in the Senate, I have attempted to indicate that this is a quality which may be found in any Senator, in any political party and in any era. Many more examples could have been mentioned as illustrative of similar conduct under similar circumstances.

Other Senators, placing their convictions ahead of their careers, have broken with their party in much the same way as John Quincy Adams, Thomas Hart Benton, Edmund Ross, Sam Houston and George Norris. The friends of Republican *Senator Albert Beveridge of Indiana* pleaded with him to soft-pedal his charges against the Payne-Aldrich Tariff Act promoted by his party in his campaign for re-election in 1910; but he would not keep silent. "A party can live only by growing," he said. "Intolerance of ideas brings its death."

An organization that depends upon reproduction only for its vote, son taking the place of the father, is not a political party, but a Chinese tong; not citizens brought together by thought and conscience, but an Indian tribe held together by blood and prejudice.

Disillusioned and discouraged when the opposition of influential segments of his own party accomplished his defeat, he had but one comment on the morning following election: "It is all right, twelve years of hard work, and a clean record; I am content."

Many of those who courageously break with their party soon find a new home in another organization. But for those who break with their section, as Senators Benton and Houston discovered, the end of their political careers is likely to be more permanent and more unpleasant. On the eve of the 1924 Democratic Convention, the advisers of *Senator Oscar W. Underwood of Alabama* — a former Presidential candidate (in 1912), a former Democratic floor leader in both the House and the Senate, author of the famous tariff bill which bore his name, and a leading Presidential possibility—urged that he say nothing to offend the Ku Klux Klan—then a rising power, particularly in Southern politics. But Senator Underwood, convinced that the Klan was contrary to all the principles of Jeffersonian democracy in which he believed, denounced it in no uncertain terms, insisted that this was the paramount issue upon which the party would have to take a firm stand, and fought vigorously but unsuccessfully to include an anti-Klan plank in the party platform. The Louisiana delegation and other Southerners publicly repudiated him, and from that moment on his chances for the Presidency were nil. He could not even be re-elected to the Senate, as Frank Kent has written:

for no other reason than the sincerity and honesty of his political utterances. . . . The opposition to him in Alabama, because of the strength and the openness of his convictions, had grown to a point where his renomination was plainly not possible without the kind of fight he felt unwilling to make. . . . Had Senator Underwood played the game in Alabama in accord with the sound political rule of seeming to say something without doing so, there would have been no real opposition to his remaining in the Senate for the balance of his life.

In those troubled days before the Civil War, great courage in opposing sectional pressures—greater perhaps even than that of Webster, Benton and Houston—was demonstrated by *Senator Andrew Johnson of Tennessee,* the bold if tactless fighter who in 1868 was saved from a humiliating ouster from the White House by the single vote of the hapless Edmund Ross. As the Union began to crack in 1860, Benton and Houston were gone from the Senate floor, and only Andrew Johnson, alone among the Southerners, spoke for Union. When his train, as he returned home to Tennessee to fight to keep his state in the Union, stopped at Lynchburg, Virginia, an angry mob dragged the Senator from his car, assaulted and abused him, and decided not to lynch him only at the last minute, with the rope already around his neck, when they agreed that hanging him was the privilege of his own neighbors in Tennessee. Throughout Tennessee, Johnson was hissed, hooted, and hanged in effigy. Confederate leaders were assured that "His power is gone and henceforth there will be nothing left but the stench of the traitor." Oblivious to the threat of death, Andrew Johnson toured the state, attempting in vain to stem the tide against secession, and finally becoming the only Southern Senator who refused to secede with his state. On his return trip to Washington, greeted by an enthusiastic crowd at the station in Cincinnati, he told them proudly: "I am a citizen of the South and of the state of Tennessee. . . . [But] I am also a citizen of the United States."

John Quincy Adams was not the only Senator

courageously to resign his seat on a matter of principle. When Andrew Jackson's personal and political popularity brought increased support for Senator Benton's long-pending measure to expunge from the *Senate Journal* the resolution censuring Jackson for his unauthorized actions against the Bank of the United States, *Senator John Tyler of Virginia,* convinced that mutilation of the *Journal* was unconstitutional and unworthy of the Senate, stood his ground. But the Virginia Legislature, dominated by Jackson's friends and Tyler's foes, and influenced by the sentimental feeling that the President should be permitted to retire without this permanent blot on his record, instructed its Senators to support the expunging resolution.

Realizing that his departure from the Senate would give the Jacksonians greater strength on far more fundamental issues, and that his own political career, which already held promise of the Vice Presidential nomination, would be at least temporarily halted, John Tyler courageously followed his conscience and wrote the legislature these memorable words:

> I cannot and will not permit myself to remain in the Senate for a moment beyond the time that the accredited organs [of] the people of Virginia shall instruct me that my services are no longer acceptable. . . .
>
> [But] I dare not touch the Journal of the Senate. The Constitution forbids it. In the midst of all the agitations of party, I have heretofore stood by that sacred instrument. The man of today gives place to the man of tomorrow, and the idols which one set worships, the next destroys. The only object of my political worship shall be the Constitution of my country. . . .
>
> I shall carry with me into retirement the principles which I brought with me into public life, and, by the surrender of the high station to which I was called by the voice of the people of Virginia, I shall set an example to my children which shall teach them to regard as nothing any position or

office which must be attained or held at the sacrifice of honor.

In one of the Senate's first outstanding demonstrations of political courage, the colorful and stormy *Senator Humphrey Marshall of Kentucky* chose in 1795 to end his career in the Senate by standing with the President in approving the immensely unpopular Jay Treaty with Great Britain. Although even the Federalists of Kentucky found it necessary to oppose President Washington on the issue, Marshall bluntly told his constituents:

> In considering the objections to this Treaty, I am frequently ready to exclaim: Ah! men of faction! friends of anarchy! enemies and willful perverters of the Federal Government! how noisy in clamor and abuse, how weak in reason and judgment, appear all your arguments!

Touring the state in defense of his vote, Marshall was shunned and stoned. Late one night a mob dragged him from his home with the avowed intention of ducking him in a nearby river. At the water's edge, United States Senator Marshall, with great calm and humor, told the raging mob:

> My friends, all this is irregular. In the ordinance of immersion as practised in the good old Baptist Church, it is the rule to require the candidate to relate his experience before his baptism is performed. Now, in accordance with established rules and precedents, I desire to give my experience before you proceed to my immersion.

Both amused and awed, the gang of unruly townspeople—few of whom knew what the Jay Treaty was, though all were convinced that Marshall had committed treason by supporting it—placed the Senator upon a stump and ordered him to explain his position. Beginning in the same humorous vein, the Senator warmed to his work and concluded his speech by caustically blistering all of his enemies, including those who stood sheepishly before him and whom he later described as poor, ignorant beings who were collected on the bank of the river for the very honorable purpose of ducking me for giving an independent opinion. Among this patriotic group, old John Byrnes, the drunken butcher, was one of the most respectable.

The freshman United States Senator from Kentucky was not "immersed"; but his sharp tongue could not prevent his involuntary retirement from the Senate.

Acts of political courage have not, of course, been confined to the floor of the United States Senate. They have been performed with equal valor and vigor by Congressmen, Presidents, Governors, and even private citizens with political ambitions. One or two examples of each are sufficient to show that neither the Senate nor Washington, D.C., has monopolized this quality.

Many years prior to his election to the Senate, *John C. Calhoun of South Carolina* demonstrated his greatest courage while a Member of the House of Representatives. When, in 1816, Congress raised its own pay from $6 a day to $1500 a year, an astounding wave of condemnation had suddenly engulfed the nation and members from all parties. Comparatively few members even dared to run for re-election. Clay narrowly avoided defeat only by the most intensive campaign of his career. Calhoun's most faithful supporters urged the young Congressman to issue a public statement promising to vote to repeal the bill if the voters would only forgive and re-elect him. But Calhoun, who once told a friend: "When I have made up my mind, it is not in the power of man to divert me," would not back down. Indeed, he suggested that perhaps $1500 was too little.

Returning to Congress vindicated by the support he had received (despite the fact that most of his former colleagues from South Carolina had been defeated for re-election), he stood practically alone on the floor of the House as Members, new and old, scrambled to denounce the bill. But not Calhoun:

> This House is at liberty to decide on this question according to the dictates of its best judgment. Are we bound in all cases to do what is popular? Have the people of this country snatched the power of deliberation from this body? Let the gentlemen name the time and place at which the people assembled and deliberated on this question. Oh, no! They have no written, no verbal instructions. The law is unpopular, and they are bound to repeal it, in opposition to their conscience and reason. If this be true, how are political errors, once prevalent, ever to be corrected?

The President of the United States is not subject to quite the same test of political courage as a Senator. His constituency is not sectional, his losses in popularity with one group or section may be offset on the same issue by his gains from others and his power and prestige normally command a greater political security than that afforded a Senator. But one example indicates that even the President feels the pressures of constituent and special interests.

President George Washington stood by the Jay Treaty with Great Britain to save our young nation from a war it could not survive, despite his knowledge that it would be immensely unpopular among a people ready to fight. Tom Paine told the President that he was "treacherous in private friendship and a hypocrite in public. . . . The world will be puzzled to decide whether you are an apostate or imposter; whether you have abandoned good principles, or whether you ever had any." With bitter exasperation, Washington exclaimed: "I would rather be in my grave than in the Presidency"; and to Jefferson he wrote:

> I am accused of being the enemy of America, and subject to the influence of a foreign country . . . and every act of my administration is tortured, in such exaggerated and indecent terms as could scarcely be applied to Nero, to a notorious defaulter, or even to a common pickpocket.

But he stood firm.

It is appropriate, in this book on the Senate, in selecting one example from among those Governors who have displayed political courage, to choose one whose brave deeds as Governor prevented him from realizing his ambition to reach the Senate. After reviewing a tremendous stack of affidavits and court records, *Governor John Peter Altgeld of Illinois* was convinced that an unfair trial and insufficient evidence had convicted the three defendants, not yet hanged, of murder in Chicago's famous Haymarket Square bombing of 1886. Warned by Democratic leaders that he must forget these convicts if he still looked toward the Senate, Altgeld replied, "No man's ambition has a right to stand in the way of performing a simple act of justice"; and when asked by the Democratic State Chairman if his eighteen-thousand-word pardon document was "good policy," he thundered, "It is right."

For his action, the Governor was burned in effigy, excluded from customary ceremonies such as parades and commencements, and assaulted daily in the press with such epithets as "anarchist," "socialist," "apologist for murder" and "fomenter of lawlessness." Defeated for re-election in 1896, denied even the customary right to make a farewell address at his successor's inaugural ("Illinois has had enough of that anarchist," the new Governor snorted), John Peter Altgeld returned to private life and a quiet death six years later. He became, in the title of Vachel Lindsay's famous poem, "The Eagle That Is Forgotten":

Sleep softly, . . . eagle forgotten, . . . under the stone,
Time has its way with you there and the clay has its own.
Sleep on, O brave-hearted, O wise man, that kindled the flame—
To live in mankind is far more than to live in a name,
To live in mankind, far, far more . . . than to live in a name.

Charles Evans Hughes in 1920 was neither a Congressman nor a Governor—but he was the most prominent lawyer in the country, a former Governor, Supreme Court Justice and Presidential nominee, and under active consideration for further public office. (He was shortly to become Secretary of State and Chief Justice.) But when five Socialists—duly elected members of a legally recognized party—were arbitrarily denied their seats in the New York State Assembly largely on the basis of their unpopular views, Hughes risked his standing and popularity to protest the action as a violation of the public's right to choose its own representatives. After a classic battle in the New York Bar Association, he succeeded in obtaining a special Association committee, with himself as chairman, to defend the Socialists—whose views he personally abhorred—before the Legislature.

Denied the right to appear in person, Hughes filed a brief insisting that "if a majority can exclude the whole or a part of the minority because it deems the political views entertained by them hurtful, then free government is at an end." His arguments apparently had little effect on the New York Legislature, which expelled the Socialists and outlawed their party. But many believe that the distinguished voice of Charles Evans Hughes, nearly alone but never afraid, and the courageous vetoes by *Governor Al Smith* of that Legislature's measures for controlling radicalism in the schools, were determining factors in arousing the nation to its senses.

To close our stories of American political courage, we would do well to recall an act of courage which preceded the founding of this nation, and which set a standard for all to follow. On the night of March 5, 1770, when an abusive and disorderly mob on State Street in Boston was rashly fired upon by British sentries, *John Adams of Massachusetts* was already a leader in the protests against British indifference to colonist grievances. He was, moreover, a lawyer of standing in the community and a candidate for the General Court at the next election. Thus, even had he not joined in the sense of shocked outrage with which all of Boston greeted the "Boston Massacre," he would nevertheless have profited by remaining silent.

But this militant foe of the Crown was asked to serve as counsel for the accused soldiers, and did not even hesitate to accept. The case, he later noted in his autobiography, was one of the "most exhausting and fatiguing causes I ever tried, hazarding a popularity very hardly earned, and incurring popular suspicions and prejudices which are not yet worn out." Yet the man who would later be a bold President—and father of an independent Senator and President—not only remained as counsel, but acquitted his clients of the murder charge, demonstrating to a packed courtroom that no evidence was at hand to show that the firing was malicious and without provocation:

> Whatever may be our wishes, our inclinations, or the dictates of our passions, they cannot alter the state of facts and evidence. The law will not bend to the uncertain wishes, imagination and wanton tempers of men. . . .
>
> Gentlemen of the Jury—I am for the prisoners at the bar; and shall apologize for it only in the words of the Marquis Beccaria: "If I can but be the instrument of preserving one life, his blessings and tears shall be sufficient consolation to me for the contempt of mankind!"

XI

THE MEANING OF COURAGE

This has been a book about courage and politics. Politics furnished the situations, courage provided the theme. Courage, the universal virtue, is comprehended by us all—but these portraits of courage do not dispel the mysteries of politics.

For not a single one of the men whose stories appear in the preceding pages offers a simple, clear-cut picture of motivation and accomplishment. In each of them complexities, inconsistencies and doubts arise to plague us. However detailed may have been our study of his life, each man remains something of an enigma. However clear the effect of his courage, the cause is shadowed by a veil which cannot be torn away. We may confidently state the reasons why—yet something always seems to elude us. We think we hold the answer in our hands—yet somehow it slips through our fingers.

Motivation, as any psychiatrist will tell us, is always difficult to assess. It is particularly difficult to trace in the murky sea of politics. Those who abandoned their state and section for the national interest—men like Daniel

Webster and Sam Houston, whose ambitions for higher office could not be hidden—laid themselves open to the charge that they sought only to satisfy their ambition for the Presidency. Those who broke with their party to fight for broader principles—men like John Quincy Adams and Edmund Ross—faced the accusation that they accepted office under one banner and yet deserted it in a moment of crisis for another.

But in the particular events set forth in the preceding chapters, I am persuaded after long study of the record that the national interest, rather than private or political gain, furnished the basic motivation for the actions of those whose deeds are therein described. This does not mean that many of them did not seek, though rarely with success, to wring advantage out of the difficult course they had adopted. For as politicians—and it is surely no disparagement to term all of them politicians—they were clearly justified in doing so.

Of course, the acts of courage described in this book would be more inspiring and would shine more with the traditional luster of hero-worship if we assumed that each man forgot wholly about himself in his dedication to higher principles. But it may be that President John Adams, surely as disinterested as well as wise a public servant as we ever had, came much nearer to the truth when he wrote in his *Defense of the Constitution of the United States:* "It is not true, in fact, that any people ever existed who love the public better than themselves."

If this be true, what then caused the statesmen mentioned in the preceding pages to act as they did? It was not because they "loved the public better than themselves." On the contrary it was precisely because they did *love themselves*—because each one's need to maintain his own respect for himself was more important to him than his popularity with others—because his desire to win or maintain a reputation for integrity and courage was stronger than his desire to maintain his office—because his conscience, his personal standard of ethics, his integrity or morality, call it what you will—was stronger than the pressures of public disapproval—because his faith that *his* course was the best one, and would ultimately be vindicated, outweighed his fear of public reprisal.

Although the public good was the indirect beneficiary of his sacrifice, it was not that vague and general concept, but one or a combination of these pressures of self-love that pushed him along the course of action that resulted in the slings and arrows previously described. It is when the politician loves neither the public good nor himself, or when his love for himself is limited and is satisfied by the trappings of office, that the public interest is badly served. And it is when his regard for himself is so high that his own self-respect demands he follow the path of courage and conscience that all benefit. It is then that his belief in the rightness of his own course enables him to say with John C. Calhoun:

> I never know what South Carolina thinks of a measure. I never consult her. I act to the best of my judgment and according to my conscience. If she approves, well and good. If she does not and wishes anyone to take my place, I am ready to vacate. We are even.

This is not to say that courageous politicians and the principles for which they speak out are always right. John Quincy Adams, it is said, should have realized that the Embargo would ruin New England but hardly irritate the British. Daniel Webster, according to his critics, fruitlessly appeased the slavery forces, Thomas Hart Benton was an unyielding and pompous egocentric, Sam Houston was cunning, changeable and unreliable. Edmund Ross, in the eyes of some, voted to uphold a man who had defied the Constitution and defied the Congress. Lucius Lamar failed to understand why the evils of planned inflation are sometimes preferable to the tragedies of uncontrolled depression. Norris and Taft, it is argued, were motivated more by blind isolationism than Constitutional principles.

All of this has been said, and more. Each of us can decide for himself the merits of the courses for which these men fought.

But is it necessary to decide this question in order to admire their courage? Must men conscientiously risk their careers only for principles which hindsight declares to be correct, in order for posterity to honor them for their valor? I think not. Surely in the United States of America, where brother once fought against brother, we did not judge a man's bravery under fire by examining the banner under which he fought.

I make no claim that all of those who staked their careers to speak their minds were right. Indeed, it is clear that Webster, Benton and Houston could not all have been right on the Compromise of 1850, for each of them, in pursuit of the same objective of preserving the Union, held wholly different views on that one omnibus measure. Lucius Lamar, in refusing to resign his seat when he had violated the instructions of his Legislature, demonstrated courage in totally opposite fashion from John Tyler, who ended his career in the Senate because he believed such instructions binding. Tyler, on the other hand, despised Adams; and Adams was disgusted with "the envious temper, the ravenous ambition and the rotten heart of Daniel Webster." Republicans Norris and Taft could not see eye to eye; and neither could Democrats Calhoun and Benton.

These men were not all on one side. They were not all right or all conservatives or all liberals. Some of them may have been representing the actual sentiments of the silent majority of their constituents in opposition to the screams of a vocal minority; but most of them were not. Some of them may have been actually advancing the long-range interests of their states in opposition to the shortsighted and narrow prejudices of their constituents;

but some of them were not. Some of them may have been pure and generous and kind and noble throughout their careers, in the best traditions of the American hero; but most of them were not. Norris, the unyielding bitter-ender; Adams, the irritating upstart; Webster, the businessmen's beneficiary; Benton, the bombastic bully—of such stuff are our real-life political heroes made.

Some demonstrated courage through their unyielding devotion to absolute principle. Others demonstrated courage through their acceptance of compromise, through their advocacy of conciliation, through their willingness to replace conflict with co-operation. Surely their courage was of equal quality, though of different caliber. For the American system of Government could not function if every man in a position of responsibility approached each problem, as John Quincy Adams did, as a problem in higher mathematics, with but a limited regard for sectional needs and human shortcomings.

Most of them, despite their differences, held much in common—the breath-taking talents of the orator, the brilliance of the scholar, the breadth of the man above party and section, and, above all, a deep-seated belief in themselves, their integrity and the rightness of their cause.

* * *

The meaning of courage, like political motivations, is frequently misunderstood. Some enjoy the excitement of its battles, but fail to note the implications of its consequences. Some admire its virtues in other men and other times, but fail to comprehend its current potentialities. Perhaps, to make clearer the significance of these stories of political courage, it would be well to say what this book is not.

It is not intended to justify independence for the sake of independence, obstinacy to all compromise or excessively proud and stubborn adherence to one's own personal convictions. It is not intended to suggest that there is, on every issue, one right side and one wrong side, and that all Senators except those who are knaves or fools will find the right side and stick to it. On the contrary, I share the feelings expressed by Prime Minister Melbourne, who, when irritated by the criticism of the then youthful historian T. B. Macaulay, remarked that he would like to be as sure of anything as Macaulay seemed to be of everything. And nine years in Congress have taught me the wisdom of Lincoln's words: "There are few things wholly evil or wholly good. Almost everything, especially of Government policy, is an inseparable compound of the two, so that our best judgment of the preponderance between them is continually demanded."

This book is not intended to suggest that party regularity and party responsibility are necessary evils which should at no time influence our decisions. It is not intended to suggest that the local interests of one's state or region have no legitimate right to consideration at any time. On the contrary, the loyalties of every Senator are distributed among his party, his state and section, his country and his conscience. On party issues, his party loyalties are normally controlling. In regional disputes, his regional responsibilities will likely guide his course. It is on national issues, on matters of conscience which challenge party and regional loyalties, that the test of courage is presented.

It may take courage to battle one's President, one's party or the overwhelming sentiment of one's nation; but these do not compare, it seems to me, to the courage required of the Senator defying the angry power of the very constituents who control his future. It is for this reason that I have not included in this work the stories of this nation's most famous "insurgents"—John Randolph, Thaddeus Stevens, Robert La Follette and all the rest—

men of courage and integrity, but men whose battles were fought with the knowledge that they enjoyed the support of the voters back home.

Finally, this book is not intended to disparage democratic government and popular rule. The examples of constituent passions unfairly condemning a man of principle are not unanswerable arguments against permitting the widest participation in the electoral process. The stories of men who accomplished good in the face of cruel calumnies from the public are not final proof that we should at all times ignore the feelings of the voters on national issues. For, as Winston Churchill has said, "Democracy is the worst form of government—except all those other forms that have been tried from time to time." We can improve our democratic processes, we can enlighten our understanding of its problems, and we can increase our respect for those men of integrity who find it necessary, from time to time, to act contrary to public opinion. But we cannot solve the problems of legislative independence and responsibility by abolishing or curtailing democracy.

For democracy means much more than popular government and majority rule, much more than a system of political techniques to flatter or deceive powerful blocks of voters. A democracy that has no George Norris to point to—no monument of individual conscience in a sea of popular rule—is not worthy to bear the name. The true democracy, living and growing and inspiring, puts its faith in the people—faith that the people will not simply elect men who will represent their views ably and faithfully, but also elect men who will exercise their conscientious judgment—faith that the people will not condemn those whose devotion to principle leads them to unpopular courses, but will reward courage, respect honor and ultimately recognize right.

These stories are the stories of such a democracy. Indeed, there would be no such stories had this nation not maintained its heritage of free speech and dissent, had it not fostered honest conflicts of opinion, had it not encouraged tolerance for unpopular views. Cynics may point to our inability to provide a happy ending for each chapter. But I am certain that these stories will not be looked upon as warnings to beware of being courageous. For the continued political success of many of those who withstood the pressures of public opinion, and the ultimate vindication of the rest, enables us to maintain our faith in the long-run judgment of the people.

And thus neither the demonstrations of past courage nor the need for future courage are confined to the Senate alone. Not only do the problems of courage and conscience concern every officeholder in our land, however humble or mighty, and to whomever he may be responsible—voters, a legislature, a political machine or a party organization. They concern as well every voter in our land—and they concern those who do not vote, those who take no interest in Government, those who have only disdain for the politician and his profession. They concern everyone who has ever complained about corruption in high places, and everyone who has ever insisted that his representative abide by his wishes. For, in a democracy, every citizen, regardless of his interest in politics, "holds office"; every one of us is in a position of responsibility; and, in the final analysis, the kind of government we get depends upon how we fulfill those responsibilities. We, the people, are the boss, and we will get the kind of political leadership, be it good or bad, that we demand and deserve.

These problems do not even concern politics alone—for the same basic choice of courage or compliance continually faces us all, whether we fear the anger of constituents, friends, a board of directors or our union, whenever we stand against the flow of opinion on strongly contested issues. For without belittling the courage with which men have died, we should not forget those acts of courage with which men—such as the subjects of this book—have *lived.* The courage of life is often a less dramatic spectacle than the courage of a final moment; but it is no less a magnificent mixture of triumph and tragedy. A man does what he must—in spite of personal consequences, in spite of obstacles and dangers and pressures—and that is the basis of all human morality.

To be courageous, these stories make clear, requires no exceptional qualifications, no magic formula, no special combination of time, place and circumstance. It is an opportunity that sooner or later is presented to us all. Politics merely furnishes one arena which imposes special tests of courage. In whatever arena of life one may meet the challenge of courage, whatever may be the sacrifices he faces if he follows his conscience—the loss of his friends, his fortune, his contentment, even the esteem of his fellow men—each man must decide for himself the course he will follow. The stories of past courage can define that ingredient—they can teach, they can offer hope, they can provide inspiration. But they cannot supply courage itself. For this each man must look into his own soul.

When, Mr. President, a man becomes a member of this body he cannot even dream of the ordeal to which he cannot fail to be exposed;
of how much courage he must possess to resist the temptations which daily beset him;
of that sensitive shrinking from undeserved censure which he must learn to control;
of the ever-recurring contest between a natural desire for public approbation and a sense of public duty;
of the load of injustice he must be content to bear, even from those who should be his friends;
the imputations of his motives;
the sneers and sarcasms of ignorance and malice;
all the manifold injuries which partisan or private malignity, disappointed of its objects, may shower upon his unprotected head.

All this, Mr. President, if he would retain his integrity, he must learn to bear unmoved, and walk steadily onward in the path of duty, sustained only by the reflection that time may do him justice, or if not, that after all his individual hopes and aspirations, and even his name among men, should be of little account to him when weighed in the balance against the welfare of a people of whose destiny he is a constituted guardian and defender.

SENATOR WILLIAM PITT FESSENDEN *of Maine,*
in a eulogy delivered upon the death of Senator Foot
of Vermont in 1866, two years before
Senator Fessenden's vote to acquit Andrew Johnson
brought about the fulfillment of his own prophecy.

BIBLIOGRAPHY

Bibliography

Note: The works of Allan Nevins and Herbert Agar are particularly helpful in commencing a study of this nature; and Haynes's history of the Senate, Cate's biography of Lamar, De Witt's recount of the Johnson impeachment, and William S. White's biography of Taft are basic reference works which have been essential to my research.—JFK

General References

(The following books were helpful in several chapters of the book or in establishing the general theme of the book in the opening and closing chapters.)

Agar, Herbert. *The Price of Union.* Boston, 1950.
Coit, Margaret L. *John C. Calhoun.* Boston, 1950.
Douglas, William O. *An Almanac of Liberty.* New York, 1954.
Gallup, George. *Public Opinion in a Democracy.* Princeton University, 1939.
Gillett, Frederick H. *George Frisbie Hoar.* Boston, 1934.

Haynes, George H. *The Senate of the United States*, Vols. 1 & 2. Boston, 1938.

Holcombe, Arthur Norman. *Our More Perfect Union; from Eighteenth-Century Principles to Twentieth-Century Practice*. Cambridge, Massachusetts, 1950.

House Doc. 607: *Biographical Directory of the American Congress*, 1774-1949. Washington, D.C., 1950.

Kent, Frank R. *Political Behavior*. New York, 1928.

Lippmann, Walter. *Essays in the Public Philosophy*. Boston, 1955.

Lowell, Abbott Lawrence. *Conflicts of Principle*. Cambridge, Massachusetts, 1932.

Luthin, Reinhard Henry. *American Demagogues: Twentieth Century*. Boston, 1954.

Malone, Dumas. *Dictionary of American Biography*. New York, 1943.

Moore, Joseph West. *The American Congress*. New York, 1895.

Morison, Samuel E., and Commager, Henry Steele. *The Growth of the American Republic*, Vols. 1 & 2. London, 1942.

Morrow, Josiah. *The Works of the Right Hon. Edmund Burke*, Vol. 2. Boston, 1894.

Nevins, Allan. *Ordeal of the Union*, Vols. 1 & 2. New York, 1947.

Nevins, Allan, and Commager, Henry Steele. *America, the Story of a Free People*. Boston, 1942.

Peterson, Houston (Ed.). *A Treasury of the World's Great Speeches*. New York, 1954.

Schlesinger, Arthur M., Jr. *The Age of Jackson*. Boston, 1946.

Turner, Julius. *Party and Constituency: Pressures on Congress*. Baltimore, 1951.

Additional References on History of the Senate and Sources for Material Contained in the Prologues to the Various Chapters

Benton, Thomas Hart. *Thirty Years' View*, 1820-1850. London and New York, 1863.

Binkley, Wilfred. *President and Congress*. New York, 1947.

Boni, Albert and Charles. *The Journal of William Maclay*. New York, published in 1890 and revised in 1927.

Brown, Everett Somerville. *William Plumer's Memorandum of Proceedings in the United States Senate, 1803-1807*. London, 1923.

Connor, R. D. W. *History of North Carolina*, Vol. 1. Chicago and New York, 1919.

Corwin, Edward. *The President, Office and Powers*, 2nd Edition. New York, 1941.

Cosgrove, Henry. "New England Town Mandates," *Publications of the Colonial Society of Massachusetts*, Vol. 21 (Transactions in 1919). Boston, 1920.

Dangerfield, Royden J. *In Defense of the Senate*. University of Oklahoma Press, 1933.

Dodd, William E. "The Principle of Instructing United States Senators," *The South Atlantic Quarterly*, Vol. 1. Durham, North Carolina, January, 1902.

Foster, Roger. *Commentaries on the Constitution of the United States*. Boston, 1895.

Galloway, George Barnes. *Congress at the Crossroads*. New York, 1946.

Harris, Joseph P. *The Advice and Consent of the Senate*. Berkeley and Los Angeles, 1953.

Haynes, George H. *The Senate of the United States*, Vols. 1 & 2. Boston, 1938.

Matthews, Donald R. "United States Senators and the Class Structure," *The Public Opinion Quarterly*, Vol. XVIII, No. 1. Princeton University, Spring, 1954.

McClendon, R. Earl. "Violations of Secrecy In Re Senate Executive Sessions, 1789-1929," *The American Historical Review*, Vol. LI. New York, October, 1945.

Miller, R., and Hoar, George F. "Has the Senate Degenerated?" *Forum*. 1897.

Moore, Joseph West. *The American Congress*. New York, 1895.

Nevins, Allan, and Commager, Henry Steele. *America, the Story of a Free People*, Boston, 1942.
Pound, Merritt B. *Benjamin Hawkins—Indian Agent*. Athens, Georgia, 1951.
Rogers, Lindsay. *The American Senate*. New York, 1926.
Smith, Goldwin. "Has the U. S. Senate Decayed?" *Saturday Review*. 1896.
Von Holst, R. "Shall the Senate Rule the Republic?" *Forum*. November, 1893.
Wilson, Woodrow. *Congressional Government*. Boston and New York, 1885.
Young, Roland. *This Is Congress*. New York, 1943.

ADDITIONAL REFERENCES FOR CHAPTER II
JOHN QUINCY ADAMS

Adams, Charles Francis. *Memoirs of John Quincy Adams* (His Diary from 1795 to 1848), Vol. 1. Philadelphia, 1874.
Adams, Henry. *New England Federalism*. Boston, 1905.
Adams, James Truslow. *The Adams Family*. Boston, 1930.
Adams, John Quincy. *Correspondence with Citizens of Massachusetts*. Boston, 1829.
Beard, Charles A. *Economic Origins of Jeffersonian Democracy*. New York, 1949.
Bemis, Samuel Flagg. *John Quincy Adams and the Foundations of American Foreign Policy*. New York, 1949.
Buckley, William. *The Hartford Convention* (Pamphlet). New Haven, Connecticut, 1934.
Clark, Bennett Champ. *John Quincy Adams*. Boston, 1932.
Dwight, Theodore. *The Hartford Convention*. Boston and New York, 1833.
Ford, W. C. "The Recall of John Quincy Adams in 1808," *Massachusetts Historical Society Proceedings*, Vol. XLV, p. 354.
Ford, Worthington Chauncey. *Writings of John Quincy Adams*, Vol. III. New York, 1914.

Hoar, George F., Representative. Speech of December 12, 1876, on dedication of statues of Samuel Adams and John Winthrop, *Congressional Record.*

Lipsky, George A. *John Quincy Adams.* New York, 1950.

Morison, Samuel Eliot. *Life and Letters of Harrison-Gray Otis,* Vols. 1 & 2. Cambridge, 1913.

Morse, Anson Ely. *The Federalist Party in Massachusetts to the Year 1800.* Trenton, New Jersey, 1909.

Morse, John T., Jr. *John Quincy Adams, American Statesmen Series,* Vol. 15. Boston and New York, 1883 and 1899.

Nevins, Allan (Ed.). *The Diary of John Quincy Adams,* 1794-1845. New York and London, 1929.

Prentiss, Hervey Putnam. *Timothy Pickering as the Leader of New England Federalism,* 1800-1815. Salem, Massachusetts, 1934.

Quincy, Josiah. *Memoir of the Life of John Quincy Adams.* Boston, 1858.

Seward, William H. *Life of John Quincy Adams.* Philadelphia, 1916.

Sullivan, William. *Public Men of the Revolution.* Philadelphia, 1847.

Wilson, Woodrow. "A Calendar of Great Americans," *Forum.* February, 1894.

Additional References for Chapter III
Daniel Webster

Adams, Samuel Hopkins. *The Godlike Daniel.* New York, 1930.

Bemis, Samuel Flagg (Ed.). *The American Secretaries of State and Their Diplomacy,* Vol. 5. Duniway, Clyde Augustus. "Daniel Webster." New York, 1928.

Benson, Allan L. *Daniel Webster.* New York, 1929.

Binkley, Wilfred E. *American Political Parties: Their Natural History.* New York, 1949.

Current, Richard. *Daniel Webster and the Rise of National Conservatism.* Boston, 1955.

Curtis, George Ticknor. *The Last Years of Daniel Webster*. New York, 1878.

Curtis, George Ticknor. *The Life of Daniel Webster*, Vols. 1 & 2. New York, 1870.

Dyer, Oliver. *Great Senators of the United States 40 Years Ago*. New York, 1889.

Fisher, Sydney George. *The True Daniel Webster*. Philadelphia and London, 1911.

Foster, Herbert Darling. *Webster's 7th of March Speech and the Secession Movement, 1850*. New York, 1922.

Fuess, Claude M. *Daniel Webster*, Vols. 1 & 2. Boston, 1930.

Harvey, Peter. *Reminiscences and Anecdotes of Daniel Webster*. Boston, 1909.

Johnson, Gerald W. *America's Silver Age*. New York, 1939.

Lanman, Charles. *The Private Life of Daniel Webster*. New York, 1852.

Lodge, Henry Cabot. *Daniel Webster, American Statesmen Series*, Vol. 21. Boston and New York, 1899.

March, Charles W. *Daniel Webster and His Contemporaries*. New York, 1859.

McClure, Col. Alexander K. *Recollections of Half a Century*. Salem, Massachusetts, 1902.

McMaster, John Bach. *Daniel Webster*. New York, 1902.

Nevins, Allan. *Ordeal of the Union*, Vols. 1 & 2. New York, 1947.

Sandburg, Carl. *Abraham Lincoln, the Prairie Years and the War Years*. New York, 1954.

Schlesinger, Arthur M., Jr. *The Age of Jackson*. Boston, 1946.

Smyth, Clifford. *Daniel Webster: Spokesman for the Union*. New York, 1931.

Van Tyne, C. H. *The Letters of Daniel Webster*. New York, 1902.

Webster, Daniel. *The Private Correspondence of Daniel Webster*. Boston, 1857.

Whittier, John G. *Whittier's Poetical Works*, "Ichabod," Vol. IV. Boston, 1888.

Wish, Harvey. *Society and Thought in Early America.* New York, 1950.

Additional References for Chapter IV
Thomas Hart Benton

Benton, Thomas Hart. *Thirty Years' View*, 1820-1850. London and New York, 1863.
Dyer, Oliver. *Great Senators of the United States 40 Years Ago.* New York, 1889.
Frémont, John Charles. *Memoirs of My Life*, Vol. 1. Frémont, Jessie Benton. "Biographical Sketch of Senator Benton, in Connection with Western Expansion." Chicago and New York, 1887.
McClure, Col. Alexander K. *Recollections of Half a Century.* Salem, Massachusetts, 1902.
McClure, Clarence Henry. *Opposition in Missouri to Benton.* Nashville, Tennessee, 1927.
McClure, Clarence Henry. "The Opposition Against Benton," *Missouri Historical Review*, Vol. 10, p. 151. State Historical Society of Missouri; Columbia, Missouri, October, 1907, and January, 1908.
Meigs, William Montgomery. *The Life of Thomas Hart Benton.* Philadelphia and London, 1904.
Rogers, Joseph M. *Thomas H. Benton.* Philadelphia, 1905.
Roosevelt, Theodore. *Thomas H. Benton.* Boston and New York, 1899.
Violette, Eugene Morrow. *History of Missouri.* Boston, 1820.
Wilson, Woodrow. "A Calendar of Great Americans," *Forum.* February, 1894.

Additional References for Chapter V
Sam Houston

Barker, Eugene C. *Mexico and Texas*, 1821-1835. Texas, 1928.
Bruce, Henry. *Life of General Houston.* New York, 1891.

Creel, George. *Sam Houston.* New York, 1928.

Culberson, Charles. "General Sam Houston and Secession," *Scribner's Magazine,* Vol. 39, 1906.

Day, Donald, and Ullom, Harry Herbert (Eds.). *The Autobiography of Sam Houston.* University of Oklahoma Press, 1954.

De Shields, James T. *They Sat in High Place.* San Antonio, 1940.

Dyer, Oliver. *Great Senators of the United States 40 Years Ago.* New York, 1889.

Evans, Gen. Clement A. *Confederate Military History,* Vol. XI. Atlanta, Georgia, 1899.

Farber, James. *Texas,* C. S. A. New York, 1947.

Friend, Llerena. *Sam Houston, The Great Designer.* University of Texas Press, 1954.

Hogan, William Ransom. *The Texas Republic, a Social and Economic History.* University of Oklahoma Press, 1946.

James, Marquis. *The Raven, a Biography of Sam Houston.* New York, 1929.

Lester, C. Edwards. *Life and Achievements of Sam Houston.* New York, 1883.

McClure, Col. Alexander K. *Recollections of Half a Century.* Salem, Massachusetts, 1902.

McGrath, Sister Paul of the Cross. *Political Nativism in Texas, 1825-1860.* Catholic University of America, 1930.

Seymour, Flora Warren. *Sam Houston, Patriot.* New York, 1930.

Smith, Justin. *The Annexation of Texas.* New York, 1911.

Sprague, Maj. J. T. *The Treachery in Texas* (The Secession of Texas and the Arrest of the United States Officers and Soldiers Serving in Texas). New York, 1862.

Weinberg, Albert K. *Manifest Destiny. A Study of Nationalist Expansionism in American History.* Johns Hopkins Press, 1935.

Winkler, William (Ed.). *Journal of the Secession Convention of Texas, 1861.* Austin, 1912.

Wortham, Louis J. *A History of Texas.* Fort Worth, 1924.

Additional References for Chapter VI
Edmund G. Ross and Those Who Stood with Him

Bowers, Claude Gernade. *The Tragic Era; The Revolution After Lincoln.* Cambridge, 1920.
Bumgardner, Edward. *The Life of Edmund G. Ross.* Missouri, 1949.
De Witt, David Miller. *The Impeachment and Trial of Andrew Johnson, Seventeenth President of the United States.* New York and London, 1903.
Dunning, Charlotte. *Essays on the Civil War and Reconstruction.* New York, 1931.
Fessenden, Francis. *Life and Public Services of William Pitt Fessenden,* Vols. 1 & 2. Cambridge, 1907.
Holzman, Robert. *Stormy Ben Butler.* New York, 1954.
Lewis, H. H. Walker. "The Impeachment of Andrew Johnson," *American Bar Association Journal.* January, 1954.
Oberholtzer, Ellis P. *A History of the United States Since the Civil War,* Vol. 2, 1868-1872. New York, 1922.
Ross, Edmund G. "History of the Impeachment of Andrew Johnson," *Forum.* July, 1895.
Ross, Edmund G. *History of the Impeachment of Andrew Johnson.* Santa Fe, 1896.
Welles, Gideon, Diary of, Vol. 3, January 1, 1867-June 6, 1869. Boston and New York, 1911.
White, Horace. *The Life of Lyman Trumbull.* Boston, 1913.

Additional References for Chapter VII
Lucius Lamar

Adams, Henry. *The Education of Henry Adams*—Autobiography. Cambridge, 1918.
Agar, Herbert. *The Price of Union.* Boston, 1950.

Blaine, James G. *Twenty Years of Congress*, Vols. 1 & 2. Norwich, Connecticut, 1884 and 1886.

Bowers, Claude Gernade. *The Outlook*, Vol. 125. New York, May-August, 1920 (July 2).

Bowers, Claude Gernade. *The Tragic Era; The Revolution After Lincoln*. Cambridge, 1920.

Cate, Wirt Armistead. *Lamar and the Frontier Hypothesis*. Reprinted from *The Journal of Southern History*, Vol. 1, No. 4. Baton Rouge, Louisiana, November, 1935.

Cate, Wirt Armistead. *Lucius Q. C. Lamar, Secession and Reunion*. Chapel Hill, 1935.

Congressional Record. February 15, 1878.

Hamilton, J. G. de Roulhac. "Lamar of Mississippi," *The Virginia Quarterly Review*, Vol. 8, No. 1. University of Virginia, January, 1932.

Hill, Walter B. "L. Q. C. Lamar," *The Green Bag*, Vol. V, No. 4. Boston, April, 1893.

Hoar, George Frisbie. *Autobiography of 70 Years*, Vols. 1 & 2. New York, 1903.

House Report 265, 43rd Congress, 2nd Session. *Vicksburg Troubles*. Washington, D.C., February 27, 1875.

Johnston, Frank. "Suffrage and Reconstruction in Mississippi," *Publications of the Mississippi Historical Society*, Vol. VI. Oxford, Mississippi, 1902.

Mayes, Edward. *Lucius Q. C. Lamar*. Nashville, Tennessee, 1896.

U. S. Supreme Court. *In Memoriam. Lucius Q. C. Lamar*. Washington, D.C., 1893.

Woods, Thomas H. "A Sketch of the Mississippi Secession Convention of 1861—Its Membership and Work," *Publications of the Mississippi Historical Society*, Vol. VI. Oxford, Mississippi, 1902.

Additional References for Chapter VIII
George W. Norris

Baker, Ray Stannard. *Woodrow Wilson, Life and Letters, 1915-1917*. New York, 1937.

Bolles, Blair. *Tyrant from Illinois: Uncle Joe Cannon's Experiment with Personal Power*. New York, 1951.

Daniels, Josephus. *The Wilson Era: Years of Peace—1910-1917*. Chapel Hill, 1944.

Hechler, Kenneth W. *Insurgency: Personalities and Politics of the Taft Era*. New York, 1940.

Lief, Alfred. *Democracy's Norris: the Biography of a Lonely Crusade*. New York, 1939.

Link, Arthur. *Woodrow Wilson and the Progressive Era: 1910-1917*. New York, 1954.

Millis, Walter. *Road to War: 1914-1917*. New York, 1935.

Mowry, George E. *Theodore Roosevelt and the Progressive Movement*. Madison, 1947.

Nebraska State Journal. March, 1917; October, 1928.

Neuberger, Richard L., and Kahn, Stephen B. *Integrity: The Life of George W. Norris*. New York, 1937.

New York *Herald Tribune*. October, 1928.

New York Times. October, 1928.

Norris, George W. *Fighting Liberal: Autobiography*. New York, 1945.

Norris, George W. *Letters*. Library of Congress Collections and files of C. A. Sorensen.

Omaha *World Herald*. March, 1917; October, 1928.

Paxson, Frederic L. *Prewar Years, 1913-1917*. Boston, 1936.

Senate and House Journals for Nebraska, 1917, 35th Session.

Tansill, Charles C. *America Goes to War*. Boston, 1938.

Additional References for Chapter IX
Robert A. Taft

Cleveland *Plain Dealer*. October 7, 8, 10, 1946.

Columbus *Dispatch*. October 8, 1946.

Harnsberger, Caroline T. *A Man of Courage*. Chicago, 1952.

New York Times. October 6, 7, 8, 9, 10, 11, 19, 24, 25, 1946.

Taft, Robert A. *A Foreign Policy for Americans*. New York, 1951.

Toledo *Blade*. October 8, 9, 14, 1946.
White, William S. *The Taft Story*. New York, 1954.

Additional References for Chapter x
Other Men of Political Courage

Bernard, Harry. *Eagle Forgotten* (The Life of John Peter Altgeld). New York, 1938.
Bowers, Claude Gernade. *Beveridge and the Progressive Era.* Cambridge, 1932.
Brown, Everett Somerville, *William Plumer's Memorandum of Proceedings in the United States Senate, 1803-1807*. London, 1923.
Chitwood, Oliver Perry. *John Tyler; Champion of the Old South*. New York, 1939.
Coit, Margaret L. *John C. Calhoun*. Boston, 1950.
Cralle, Richard K. *Reports and Public Letters of John C. Calhoun*, Vol. 2. New York, 1855.
Fraser, Hugh Russell. *Democracy in the Making*. Indianapolis and New York, 1938.
Hapgood and Moskowitz. *Up from the City Streets: Alfred E. Smith*. New York, 1927.
Kent, Frank R. *Political Behavior*. New York, 1928.
Marshall, Humphrey. *History of Kentucky*, Vol. 2. Frankfort, Kentucky, 1824.
Morgan, Robert J. *A Whig Embattled; the Presidency under John Tyler*. Lincoln, 1954.
New York Times. January 26, 1929.
Pusey, Merlo J. *Charles Evans Hughes*, Vols. 1 & 2. New York, 1951.
Quisenberry, A. C. *The Life and Times of Hon. Humphrey Marshall.* Winchester, Kentucky, 1892.
Simms, Henry H. *The Rise of the Whigs in Virginia.* Richmond, Virginia, 1929.
Stoddard, William O. *John Adams, the Lives of the Presidents*, Vol. 2. New York, 1886.
Stryker, Lloyd Paul. *Andrew Johnson, A Study in Courage*. New York, 1929.
Underwood, Oscar W. *Drifting Sands of Party Politics.* New York, 1928.
Washington *Evening Star*. January 25, 1929.

Index